Designs for a New Age
Rectangles and Yods

Rev. Alice Miller, LMAFA

ISBN-10: 0-86690-649-5
ISBN-13: 978-0-86690-649-4

Cover Design: Jack Cipolla

Published by:
American Federation of Astrologers, Inc.
6535 S. Rural Road
Tempe, AZ 85283

www.astrologers.com

Printed in the United States of America

Books by Rev. Alice Miller

The Lunar Nodes to Pars Fortuna: Journey and Goal
Designs for a New Age: Rectangles and Yods
Heralds of a New Age: Interceptions
Possibilities for a New Age: Intercepted Planets
Pagan Astrology for the Spirit and Soul

The following books are available from www.lifeprintastroloy.com
Principles of Astrology: Planets, Signs and Houses
Dynamics of Astrology: Interpreting Aspects
Soul of Astrology: Inner Dimensions of the Modern Moon
Retrograde Planets and Consciousness
Astrology's Kabbalistic Vision of Human Life
Healing the Inner Child: The Astrology of Family Dysfunction
Getting Birth Charts on Target

About the Author

Alice Miller was born in the Kansas farm country during the Great Depression. The oldest of five children, she was expected to be both Mother's helper and Dad's farmhand. She left home and became self-supporting at age sixteen.

Conditioned to keep busy and work hard, she married early and reared four children, almost single-handedly. Although she worked at a variety of jobs to keep the family together, she considered herself a professional waitress.

At her Uranus opposition, she began studying astrology, becoming a part-time professional six years later. At her Saturn return, she retired from the national work force to a full-time professional practice including counseling, teaching, and writing in the field of astrology.

Today, Rev. Miller resides in the Denver, Colorado area, from which, through her website, www.lifeprintastrology.com, she reaches out to a worldwide practice. Although she no longer teaches, she continues to write, and through her writings to teach some of the new methods and insights she has developed in more than thirty years of practice. Some of those books are self-published and only available from her website. Several others, published by AFA, are available from AFA and from www.amazon.com.

In addition, Rev. Miller maintains an online newsletter, Spirit and Stars. She is always happy to hear from readers at astrominister1@yahoo.com, with comments or questions or requests to be added to the mailing list for Spirit and Stars.

Contents

Introduction

As consciousness rises among the people, it becomes increasingly clear that aspects within the horoscope act negatively only within the individual's ego programming. Although at the spiritual level there is no internal conflict, many are trying to resolve conflicts between their essential being and their conditioning. Natal horoscopes hold useful keys to doing so. The modern astrologer teaches clients to handle their aspects in ways that adapt early childhood conditioning to promote spiritual and personal growth.

An opposition is comprised of one or more planets or points placed approximately 180 degrees from another planet, point, pair, or cluster of planets. Oppositions show conflicts in our life instructions. Sometimes these represent conflicts between adults in our childhood. Other times they show conflicts in the messages given us.

Even when there are no planets in opposition, every chart has an opposition between the Ascendant and Descendant, between the IC and Midheaven, and between the North and South Nodes; so the study of opposing energy constructs can benefit everyone.

The opposition aspect has the nature of Libra. The two ends must learn to cooperate or fight. If they can create a successful marriage, they will function much like a conjunction, peacefully and together. However, many oppositions argue from the basis of beliefs in the general consciousness. To give you the idea of the kind of conflicts shown by oppositions, here are some beliefs held in the past that sometimes spill their discomfort into the present:

1. Women belong at home.

    a. They may work before marriage and/or after their children are grown.

    b. They should not expect to have a real career, nor take a job that is needed by a man who is, after all, the family breadwinner.

2. To feel successful, a woman must be married.

3. To feel successful, a woman must have children.

4. Real men like sports and physical pursuits.

5. Real men leave the housework and children to their wives

6. Men must marry.

7. Men must father heirs, especially sons, to carry on the family name.

The above notions were listed because they are some of the most persistent areas of conflict in the psyche of the general consciousness. For generations they have been used to create sharp divisions between males and females. As we begin to recognize the basic similarity of qualities within males and females, the sharpness of the division between them is being dulled. However, with several major religions still promoting these or similar beliefs, they continue to hang over many people, shadowing their lives from the subconscious.

The local economy, with its necessity for almost all people to be self-supporting during some portion of their lives is helping to modify these prejudices. Stay-at-home mothers are becoming as obsolete as dinosaurs because two incomes are usually necessary to support a family. This has forced many to take a new look at marriage and child rearing, deferring it until late in life or abstaining altogether. At the same time, better education for everyone has meant that women have learned to exercise minds that were once encouraged to shut down at puberty.

Thinking people realize that the world population has already reached and surpassed optimum levels. There is no further rationale to the ancient command to "go forth and populate the Earth." Overpopulation in certain areas has already led to starvation and premature death for millions. Infertile unions are thus becoming increasingly popular, but with those old religious imperatives still pervading the atmosphere of many homes where children are growing up, the oppositions between what we are taught to believe and what we naturally and rationally think continue to cause internal stress to many. This kind of conflict stands behind most oppositions in natal charts.

Upside-down Charts

You will see some upside-down charts in this book. In fact, you'll find the first one in the first chapter on Rectangles. Why? No, it is not the editor; it is me, the author. Here is the story.

The first book I wrote was never published and the manuscript was eventually lost. It was called "Seventh House as Self-Realization" and its thesis was that we need to begin to reclaim our Descendant and seventh house as the back side of our Ascendant and first house. They are both part of our self-image, but looking in a mirror we can only see the front, i.e., the Ascendant. So traditionally, the Descendant and seventh house went unclaimed and were projected on others.

I wrote, "The Ascendant is like your right hand. You use it to reach for things. When you do, you do not hold your left hand behind you. You use it to assist the right hand. So the Descendant should be used to assist the Ascendant, for even though you cannot see it in the mirror, it is still a part of you."

Writing that, I had one of those *aha* moments that strike like a blinding flash of light.

What about people who *reach for life* with their left hand? Could their Ascendant be on the officially descending side of the chart? My family is well supplied with lefties so I had several charts to try the idea on and it seemed valid. I began asking clients for hand dominance, and turning the charts of lefties 180 degrees, or upside-down. Within the first few months I was gifted with the opportunity to re-read the charts of several lefties who had received less-than-optimal readings from other astrologers . . . and I got rave reviews.

I often tell students that the hardest chart to read accurately is their own. We see what we think should be there rather than what is there. In my own case, I had been struggling with my own chart for several years, but even as I gained more experience it still did not make sense.

Then one day, my left shoulder was really sore. I could not discover why or what to do about it. I kept thinking about a story told by my mother. We lived in a house with a cellar and the cellar door was in the floor. When I was about 18 months old, I walked off the edge and fell into the cellar. Thinking about the sore shoulder, I wondered whether I might have incurred an unnoticed injury to that shoulder just at the time when my hand dominance was being established. It seemed reasonable because my left eye is much stronger than the right.

I asked several psychic friends about this possibility. They all concurred with my hunch. I then went home, turned my own chart over, and suddenly it made perfect sense!

Since that day, when I learn that someone has a noticeably stronger left eye, I turn that chart as well. Again with good results.

Astrology has long recognized that left-handed people tend to be more intuitive than right-handed ones. People who are left-brained (logic dominant) have right physical dominance—they are born right handed. People who are born right-brained (intuitive dominant) are born with left physical dominance.

More in the past than in the present, it was common practice to force the lefties to the right, so they would better fit-in. I have come to believe that clients who are nominally right-handed but have a significantly stronger left eye have had their hand-dominance changed early in life. As a corollary, most are also dyslexic because of the confused wiring in the brain. It is natural for them to reach for life with the left hand, but they are conditioned to ignore it and reach with the right. This can cause damage to the ability to learn in traditional school situations.

The one gift, available to these people is that some of them eventually develop whole-brain thinking—a condition that is occurring naturally in some, possibly all, of today's children.

Part I

Rectangles

Introduction

Every chart contains at least three oppositions: the horizon, the meridian, and the nodal axis. Rectangles formed by the angles between any two of these are the easiest ones to spot.

The commonest of these is a Grand Cross, or Grand Square, formed by the angle between the horizon (Ascendant-Descendant) and meridian (Midheaven-IC). The houses[1] in any chart wheel are environmental factors. The meridian is, essentially, a time line; the horizon is a spacial line. The point at the center of the chart where the two cross marks the actual location in time-space where the birth of the person occurred.

Natal charts with an Ascendant-Midheaven angle of ninety degrees (orb about five degrees) have a particular meaning. This Grand Cross has the feel of time and space being *out of sync.*

When these individuals make appointments to meet someone, they tend to find themselves habitually arriving early or late. Alternatively, they may be *spatially handicapped* so that, although they arrive on time, they arrive at the wrong place. Any form this *disability* takes can be annoying to the point where the expectation of repetition tends to recreate it time after time.

The cure for this frustrating problem is knowledge. The spiritual meaning of this chart marker is simple. You are one whose life is being directed by higher mind, and it is responsible for the *apparent mistakes.* They are, in fact, not mistakes at all. Know this: You are always in the right place at the right time, having been guided there for some specific reason which you may or may not ever know. In some instances, what happens keeps you out of a dangerous situation. In other instances, you are taken to a point in time-space where your presence is needed, as in a particular location or to meet a particular person.

Once you fully understand the truth of this, you can stop worrying about the time or destination of your meetings. When you do, you will discover something interesting. When you arrive

---

[1]In any house system other than the equal house system. (The equal house system is of doubtful usefulness.)

late, so does the other person. When you arrive *early*, so does the other person. And if you go to the *wrong place*, so does the other person. Your *problem* has resolved itself into a gift.

The second easiest Rectangle to see is one formed by the nodal axis and either the horizon or meridian of a chart. These point to a relationship between your evolutionary intent and your birth location. A positive aspect, especially a trine, sextile, quintile, or decile, is an obvious gift. Negative aspects like quadrates and inconjuncts show apparent difficulties in synchronizing the physical and spiritual goals. Other aspects show varying relationships to your *time of birth* or *place of birth*. Know that the time issues will be resolved by time, while the space issues are more easily resolved by a change of residence–specifically some distance east or west.

Most of all, do not become invested in apparent *problems* involving difficult aspects between the nodal axis and either the horizon or meridian. You can be certain that these elements were figured into your life-plans for this incarnation. You, and the spirit within you, did and do know what it is all about. To quote Marcus Bach:

> Every problem carries a gift in its hands.

Look for your gift. Expect your gift. In doing so you will create it and/or draw it into your life.

Analyzing the Opposition

Oppositions usually pit water signs against earth signs or fire signs against air signs.[2] A little common sense will reveal that without water, earth cannot grow anything, and without air, fire will not burn. Notice also that without earth–something to contain it–water runs all over, accomplishing little. No amount of intelligence, without some desire to fire it, will be retained. The essential conflict in oppositions originates with a belief, not a truth.

I was born with an excellent mind. Growing up in the 1940s, I was constantly reminded that my good grades would mean little when I was grown because I was destined only to be a wife and mother. I have Capricorn on the third and fourth house cusps, with Cancer on the ninth and tenth. Jupiter in Capricorn at the IC opposes Pluto in Cancer at the Midheaven. Those statements implied that wisdom was useless because it could not be empowered by the very public tenth house Pluto–due to my gender. I never entirely believed this, but was compelled to marry and rear four children before becoming a professional astrologer and writer. More than that, I married a somewhat immature man who could not be transformed into my idea of what a husband and father should be.

Every natural opposition is between two signs of the same mode. Two cardinal points are both active. Two fixed points are both passive. Two mutable points are both conscious. The general rule for the cardinal opposition is simple: Get them both headed in the same direction and they will cooperate nicely. Aries can fire Libra's love into passion, producing creativity. Capricorn can shape Cancer's nurture to a specific project for the achievement of a goal.

Probably the most difficult oppositions are the fixed ones. Fixed points pull energy and if the two of them continually pull on each other, the opposition tends to be locked in place. If Scorpio tries to transform what Taurus is building, destruction is often the result. If they both realize that

---

[2]For greater understanding until you design a special use for them, treat out-of-sign oppositions as quincunxes and say that they won't work together.

Scorpio can be used to dig the foundation, or to adapt the building site, then Taurus can build successfully. If Taurus will allow it, Scorpio can invest its earnings for greater profit. Similarly, if Leo and Aquarius can understand the principles of action-reaction, much can be accomplished at both ends. Here Leo must act in such a way as to get the desired reaction from Aquarius. They must act in the same drama and realize that if the Leo star wants recognition from the Aquarian audience, the play must be about something worthy of Aquarian attention.

The spiritual aspect often enters into this opposition as Leo's personal role is one that dramatizes an impersonal or cosmic principle, thus becoming an impersonal one. When we get personal satisfaction from doing something for the world or for the future, we have balanced this axis. Where there is a fixed opposition, we must discover a way to get the two ends of the axis to cooperate. They can literally feed each other and *share the food* when they learn not to be greedy.

The mutable or conscious opposition must learn to divide the labor and choose priorities. Each end of the axis has the capacity to both feed energy like a cardinal point and receive energy like a fixed one. Cooperation is quite simple. The active side of the right point feeds the passive side of the left, and the passive side of the right is fed by the active side of the left, producing a criss-cross pattern. Alternatively, the matter of priorities can be addressed. What Gemini learns, Sagittarius can teach, and teaching will learn more. What Virgo analyzes, Pisces can master, leading to perfect function based on subconscious memory patterns.

Ultimately, the mission of cardinal signs is to move us forward, while the mission of fixed signs is to maintain the integrity of that which is in motion. Meanwhile, mutable signs are the means of raising consciousness as they discover the interaction between active and passive energies and learn to manipulate them for greater efficiency. Whenever an opposition exists, the opportunity for greater internal cooperation, integrity and growth is offered. With the oppositions understood, we can go on to discover what special opportunities the configurations based on oppositions represent and how they can be made to serve our personal and spiritual growth.

Most oppositions must be resolved individually before the full benefit of the rectangular configuration can be realized. When one opposition lies within an interception, we are given a clear mandate to resolve the other one first. It always takes time to make intercepted areas conscious and this will be especially true of an intercepted opposition, partly because the interception shows an unconscious conflict.

Because of this, the aspects between the points of the two oppositions cannot function until at least one side of the interception has been transited by an outer planet. This makes the interception conscious, allowing us to resolve its issues. With that completed, suddenly the configuration hands us an entirely new talent or opportunity. Without the interception, the process is similar but more gradual. We may work on the construct over a long period, gradually releasing the several elements represented by the different planetary linkages until the last *piece of the puzzle* slips into its proper place.

Magic Rectangle
Creative Consciousness 72-108°

The quintile aspect has long been associated with creativity, but only now, with the upsurge of awareness in the general population, has it opened to real understanding. This aspect might once have been called the mark of the magician. Today it shows an innate ability to create and recreate our own reality. The tredecile is equal to three deciles or one and one-half quintiles. Requiring activation, like any decile, it points to the resistance that makes us aware of a need for superhuman abilities. Need is the magnetic force that lifts our attention to the abilities latent in our spiritual heritage. In times of crisis we call on powers that we ignore during more peaceful periods.

With the appearance of the modern personal computer, we have a visual symbol of the human consciousness structure. Computers run on resistance, providing a symbolic clue to the way in which adversity motivates a rise in human consciousness. The Magic Rectangle pictures one driven to remember and use ritual magic or scientific prayer.

Lisa

First Natal Opposition

In Lisa's chart the basic Rectangle is comprised of the horizon and meridian. Initially, every horizon opposes the self-image with the other-image. This horizontal split is derived from a family world view that splits the population into those who own/Taurus and those who control/Scorpio. The split is essentially between money and power; it takes the control of money away from its owners. The underlying message is to marry for money, and to control the marital assets. A hidden asset of this polarity is that Scorpio rules the principle of fusion, and as it evolves it naturally fuses with Taurus. The personal values of Taurus become invested in the impersonal values of Scorpio and begin producing interest—money and/or rising consciousness.

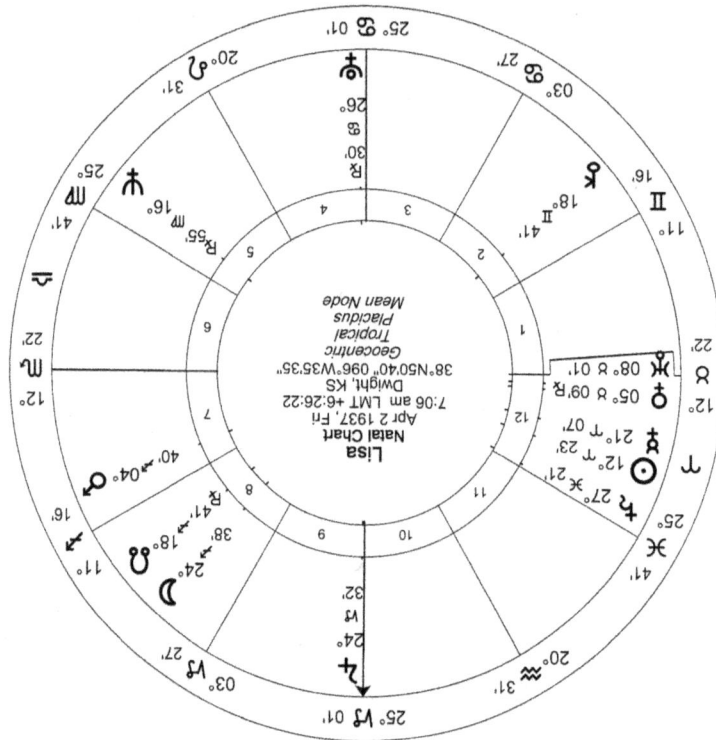

Lisa
Natal Chart
Apr 2 1937, Fri
7:06 am LMT +6:26:22
Dwight, KS
38°N50'40" 096°W35'35"
Geocentric
Tropical
Placidus
Mean Node

At the Descendant Uranus is conjunct retrograde Venus, ruler of the seventh, opposing the Ascendant. The nature of retrograde Venus in Taurus is to value the physical as an expression of the spiritual. Lisa knows that love is not an action; it is a state of being. Venus conjunct Uranus describes unconditional love, a universal principle that values/Taurus all life equally, without conditions.

As a child, one *name* she was called was "no-good"; another was "worthless." This directly conflicts with her in-born attitude of universal love. She knew that she was not worthless, but felt the need to prove that her version of love had value for the world. She sought approval, first from family, then from mates. Eventually she realized that impersonal love gets approval only from other impersonal/transpersonal beings.

The opposition from Uranus to the Ascendant shows that her self-image was confronted by insanity. Her childhood was saturated by messages that devalued females–they were good for nothing except being wives and mothers. Even so, the family business manager and the actual head of the family was her powerful, controlling mother. The only real resistance to Mother's power came from an equally powerful paternal grandmother. Basing her female image on them clearly identifies Lisa as powerful/Scorpio, but her power is love, not control.

Second Opposition

The meridian is the time line, with birth at the IC and full maturation at the Midheaven. The split suggests that you cannot get there from here. It implies reincarnation and that which was excluded from the family belief system. With the signs reversed from their natural position, the necessary progress is from maturation to innocence. Lisa often comments that she is living her life in reverse because as the years pass she becomes younger and younger in spirit.

Capricorn refers to the limits of the current definition of humankind. Chart factors in Capricorn are up against the ceiling of what is generally believed possible to the human species. They seem to have no place to go and grow. Only when we understand that Saturn's limits are always temporary and intended to be pushed outward by Jupiter, do we realize that we can cross our boundaries and exceed our limits. In Capricorn, that means exceeding what is generally believed to be *possible to humans*. The Cancer Midheaven, especially when conjunct Pluto, points to a rebirth beyond the traditional definition of humankind. The conjunction of Jupiter to the IC guarantees growth. A single Capricorn planet is the "chart manager" and its place at the base of the chart shows foundation. All that happens will proceed from the mature wisdom present at birth.

The issue of time is reemphasized by the Jupiter-Pluto opposition. In the consciousness structure, Jupiter serves as our CPU[3] and this one begins life at the gateway that takes conceptual understanding to the next level. The opposition is from a very young Cancer Pluto.[4] Jupiter cannot move on until Pluto *catches up*–again, a matter of time and maturity.[5]

Metaphysically, Pluto represents the ability to use Uranus and Neptune consciously, deliberately manipulating attention to achieve goals. Pluto is the key *New Age* planet, representing the creative power of the word. We cannot control our reality until we learn to use Pluto power as a creative force. Placing Pluto at the top of the chart shows a life goal of deliberately engineered rebirth. It also shows feminine power hanging over Lisa's head, forcing her to claim it or pay the price for not doing so. She is like a larva whose consciousness is directed toward the goal of getting off the ground on butterfly wings.

Ascendant-IC Quintile

The quintile from the Ascendant to the IC easily blends the power of Scorpio with the rights and responsibilities of Capricorn. Because of her innate spiritual maturity, Lisa has the moral right to do anything she has the power/ability to do. Jupiter combines well with the IC, as both inner and outer understanding. She naturally understands the physical application of spiritual principles. Her position is "in the world" but not "of the world."

---

[3]Central Processing Unit, which does computer calculations. The capacity for deductive reasoning.
[4]Lisa was born just seven years after the discovery of Pluto, so the Pluto principle was unrecognized in the world of her childhood.
[5]Please note that Jupiter rules the North Node and Pluto rules the Ascendant. See the previous chapter for delineation of the way the inborn level of consciousness relates to the self-image.

IC-Descendant Tredecile

The tredecile from IC to Descendant points to the achievement of money and approval, but only after the two oppositions are resolved. The meridian must center between the past and future, bringing the farsighted vision of Jupiter into present reality. When her focus moves to the center of the chart, the abilities of Venus, Uranus, Jupiter, and Pluto will combine as a powerful expression of impersonal love that will automatically attract approval and money. Activation of the second quadrant by Saturn and Uranus transits was designed to force Lisa to look inward.

Venus-Uranus at the Descendant initially left them unclaimed as "not me." Lisa was never really a girl/maiden. When Venus, ruler of the seventh, backed into her Aries interception, it seemed to take her hopes of rising above her conditioning with it. The inherited female role must be fulfilled first. A loaded sixth house gives Lisa the ability to do many things at once. Becoming a wife and mother very early in life, she reared four children almost single-handedly, while battling her own abuse issues. As Saturn made its first return and crossed the sixth house, she struggled with issues of work and deteriorating health, while her first marriage came apart. Ten years later, she experienced another concentrated series of events as Uranus opposed Venus, its own natal place, and crossed the Ascendant. While recovering from a chronic depression, she went through successful surgery for uterine cancer, and the following year became the sole support of the family when her disabled second husband lost his pension.

After that, the last of her children left home, followed by another divorce. During the same period, looking for an explanation for her chaotic life, she discovered metaphysics and began to study astrology. Years later she realized the magnitude of what she had accomplished under unusually difficult conditions. At forty-five she emerged from the battlefield like a woman carrying a newborn infant, born under a bombardment of bullets.

Only later did she recognize that personal power, magic, or miracle as the only logical explanations for her survival and continued growth under incredible pressure. One day she would write about rebirth as preceded by an often difficult pregnancy and labor period.

Descendant-Midheaven Quintile

The quintile from Descendant to Midheaven points to the female image,[6] but the essence of femininity lies in the retrograde Taurus Venus. Of the retrograde condition we say that the feminine role is familiar and comfortable. Uranus makes this role a kind of abstraction so that it ultimately refers to the feminine principles. While Lisa likes being a female, she is definitely a not-traditional one.

During her early years the Descendant stellium was essentially out of the picture and she was

---

[6]Although Lisa's foundation belief is Christ-centered, the four points of this configuration are most clearly defined by Wicca's triple goddess: the Capricorn Crone, the Taurus Maiden, the Cancer Mother focus through the Scorpio Witchwoman Ascendant.

left with a public image as a powerful/Pluto mother/Cancer. Because of it she attracted dependent, mother-dominated men, who added to her burdens and interrupted her spiritual progress.

As Uranus opposed the then squared areas, she was briefly married to and divorced from first, a physical abuser, and later an emotional abuser. Between the two incidents the biggest transformative period of her life was triggered by a partnership with and betrayal by her oldest son. By now she could see beyond appearances and notice the beneficial side effects of each episode. She lost her fear of crises, realizing that she was using these incidents to drive her awareness deeper and higher. Although the pressure of each event was intense, the duration of them was much shorter than during earlier years. Moving past her second Saturn return and waning Uranus square, she began to understand the amazing power that moves magically through her life, and she is learning to use it with intention.

Midheaven-Ascendant Tredecile

The final tredecile is from the Midheaven to the Ascendant. The Midheaven essentially refers to the second Saturn return, marking the time when attention moves to retirement from our social period. It marked Lisa's retirement from the job arena to a full-time career as an astrologer and writer. With Pluto just beyond it, we know that soon after that the motherly public image would be transformed, initially remodeled into a grandmotherly/crone image because Venus is still intercepted and must function through Pluto. However, Venus would progress out of interception as transiting Neptune formed a sextile with her natal Venus-Uranus during her sixty-fourth year, in time for the official retirement age of sixty-five. Perhaps she can recover Venus' maiden image, moving gracefully into the twenty-first century.[7]

---

[7]This was originally written in 1999.

Grand Cross

A natural Grand Cross pits the elements in a particular mode against each other each other. Each square represents a planet and sign that *trips up* the next. Progress along life's path is exceedingly difficult when we keep stumbling over our own feet.

The square represents interference. Planets in opposition are *across the table* from each other. Although on opposite sides of an issue, they can see each other clearly. The square aspect puts the planets at right angles to each other, requiring us to turn to face them. Turning toward any planet in the cross, blocks our view of other elements. When we begin work on one opposition, the other distracts us. Staying focused on either long enough to achieve resolution is difficult.

The following two example charts each have a Grand Cross/Square behind the Rectangle. Because of this, there are two examples of the configuration–one fixed, one cardinal.

Liz

Liz has a fixed Grand Cross superimposed over her Mystic Rectangle; it pits all the passive signs against each other. These signs all draw energy and the design shows conflict in the need system. The configuration keeps the planets that define it struggling for attention/energy as each tries to take from the other, throwing the entire system out of balance. Liz's Grand Cross is a classic one in that opposing planets are also in natural pairs. In her, the very principle of the configuration must be resolved. It is all about living *on the Earth*, not *of the Earth*. Liz is a truly Universal being, channeling great wisdom to Earth.

First Opposition: Moon-Saturn

Moon opposition Saturn is a split between nurture and discipline, which also splits feelings and responses. The internal conflict is based on the value of nurture and discipline in relationships.

From the first-seventh house polarity, this opposition is in the same signs as the horizon, which

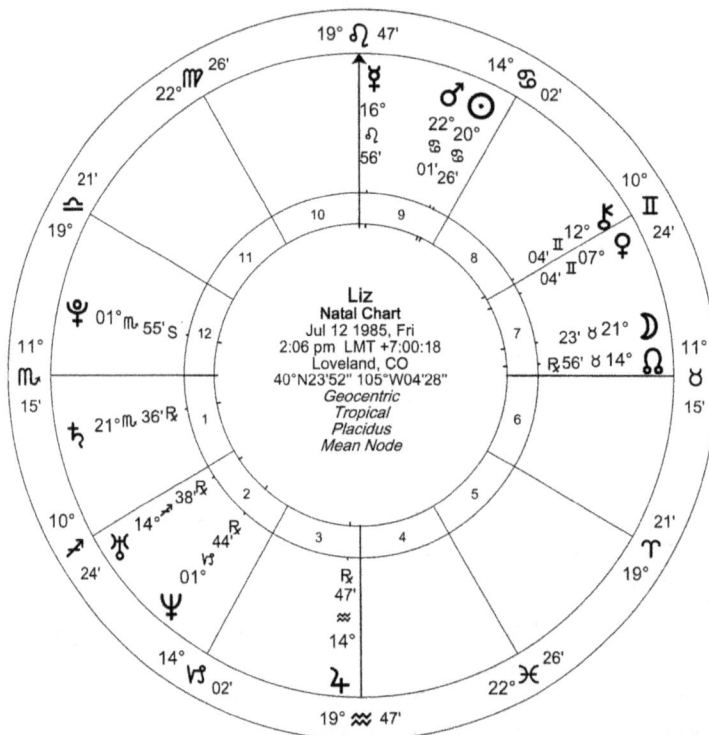

Liz
Natal Chart
Jul 12 1985, Fri
2:06 pm LMT +7:00:18
Loveland, CO
40°N23'52" 105°W04'28"
Geocentric
Tropical
Placidus
Mean Node

is the issue being focused through the planets. The parental world view divided the have-nots/Scorpio from the haves/Taurus, with a focus on the Moon/nurture and Saturn/discipline. Mom was at home, running the household, while a very conservative dad was away making money.

Liz's mother comes from a background that is rich in nurture but lacking in discipline. Her father comes from a single-parent home where nurture took the form of discipline. Their differing parenting style created conflicts in their relationship that drained them both. Early in life, this conflict became internalized in Liz, set in place by the nodal axis.

Evaluation was a lifestyle for both parents, and it came out strangely. The mother, a biological parent to two girls, strongly favored Liz, while the father, who had adopted her sister, treated them equally. Early in life Liz tended to take advantage, but as she matured she became increasingly angry at her mother for playing favorites. That anger added fuel to her teenage rebellion.

The gift in this opposition is that Saturn is retrograde, manifesting more as responsiveness than responsibility. Although she is empathic and naturally sensitive to the needs of others, the first house Saturn trine the ninth house Mars-Sun will fuse Scorpio responsibility for herself with Saturn's responsiveness. As she matures this will allow her to merge her own needs with those of others in a way that serves both a personal and an impersonal purpose.

Part I: Rectangles

Second Opposition: Mercury-Jupiter

The second opposition is Leo Mercury opposition Aquarius Jupiter. Placed in the tenth and fourth houses, the opposition directs considerable attention to family beliefs. Her father was reared a protestant fundamentalist and her mother was reared a Catholic. Liz was reared nominally Catholic, but without much spiritual emphasis.

With Jupiter and Uranus in mutual reception and Mars conjunct her Sun, Liz has a natural rebellious streak, and her teen years were trying for both Liz and her parents. As Liz approached puberty, almost simultaneously her previously possessive/Taurus mother suddenly let go,[8] giving her total responsibility for herself. With her mother in a state of change, Dad's attention was riveted on Mom, so Liz felt completely abandoned–apparently by the circumstances.

Since Uranus rules Jupiter's sign, in time the circumstances provided an opening for an Aquarian teacher to step in, helping Liz to reconnect Jupiter's much higher mind with the personal mind of Mercury.

Interestingly enough, with Jupiter retrograde, Liz must find or create her own belief system. This opposition emphasizes that the Mercury/questions get no Jupiter/answers, or at least none that made sense to her. As a teen she resolved it for herself by joining a Wicca Coven.

First Square: Jupiter-Moon

The inborn wisdom of the Aquarius Jupiter as the foundation planet of the chart is powered from outside the Solar System.[9] Aquarius is universal, eternal and unconditional. This Jupiter is extraordinarily wise and that wisdom is related to Liz's incarnational intent. Although Aquarius is a fixed sign, the only thing *fixed* about Aquarius is change, so it does not *pull energy* through aspects to other planets in the way that other fixed signs do. Technically, it draws energy from sources beyond the solar system.

Outwardly, Jupiter is the conceptual function and traditionally has not been expected to function in small children. However, Liz is a New Kid. As a small child she often knew things that startled her parents. When asked how she knew them, she would say, "I figured it out."

Second Square: Moon-Mercury

The second square is Moon-Mercury. In the child, mother's feelings draw attention away from Liz's questions. Because of the sensitive retrograde Saturn, Liz can *read people* and knows things she cannot explain. She learns not to ask questions because of the way it makes her mother feel. Early in life she learned to suppress much of what she knew.

---

[8]Liz was about ten when Uranus began to tranist opposition a seven-planet stellium in her mother's chart. The mother has a natal Uranus-Saturn trine so at this transit she began breaking all her own rules.
[9]Her Neptune at 1 Capricorn is conjunct the Galactic Center.

Third Square: Mercury-Saturn

The third square is Mercury-Saturn. Scorpio Saturn refers to *fused boundaries* and shows that she has absorbed some of her mother's rules. However, the retrograde condition and the trine to Mars-Sun show that she applies them differently, making them her own.

A key element is that her Sun is Cancer, so she is like her Cancer father, although her Leo Mercury thinks like Leo mother. The passive Moon pulls energy from the active Sun, but Mars will protect the Sun by applying raw survival energy. This forces Saturn and the Moon to share energy, creating a self-limiting channel by means of the Saturn-Moon merger. We say that the conjunction mediates the opposition.

The second key is Venus. She is mutable and can feed both Mercury and Jupiter, mediating that opposition. Venus in Gemini is the value of consciousness and she understands that Love and Light are really one. Metaphysically, our Deity is both a God of Love and a Universal Intelligence. At the personal level, love can be transmitted consciously, as the gift of teaching.

Fourth Square: Saturn-Jupiter

The fourth square is Saturn-Jupiter. To all appearances the responsiveness to her mother modifies Liz's responsiveness to the vast wisdom of Jupiter so that it gets no energy, no attention. The outer effect of this is shown by the retrograde condition of Jupiter. Placed in Aquarius, Jupiter's retrograde condition simply refers to abilities developed *off-world* or before the beginning of this lifetime and brought in with her. Here the evolutionary level is very high and its frequency must be lowered to bring it into manifestation at this time. Gradually, as the general consciousness rises, the incredible wisdom of her Jupiter can begin to *shine like the star that it is.*

Joshua

A cardinal cross represents an image problem. The four arms of this cross represent the personal I, the private/family I, the impersonal/other I, and the public/future I. Energized for action, when the cardinal signs are pitted against each other we must first discover who is acting before we can know how we are designed to act or express the divinity within us. This example shows active signs placed in passive houses. Conditioned to remain fixed by their house positions, the planets gather energy until they quite literally burst the Saturnian limitations of childhood to become something quite different from what the parents had planned. This is a prime example of using resistance to power growth in consciousness.

Joshua's growth Rectangle and Grand Cross share an intercepted opposition, so the two configurations would be resolved together, after he became an adult. The configurations found their resolution following his Uranus opposition, when he finally married. After that, one church satisfied his need for a base belief system and another taught him how to use his psychic gift.

Joshua
Natal Chart
Dec 17 1909, Fri
3:45 pm LMT +6:17:16
Alfsborg, MN
44°N30' 094°W19'
Geocentric
Tropical
Placidus
Mean Node

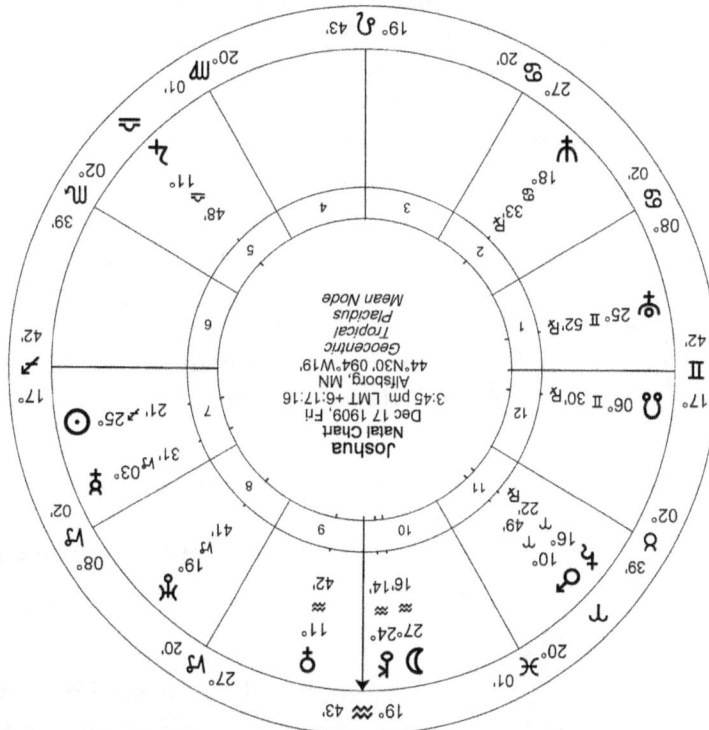

First Opposition: Uranus-Neptune

Time heals Cancer-Capricorn oppositions. With the mature Capricorn Uranus placed in the second house, we know that Joshua's ability to adapt to, or change, circumstances is his most valuable personal asset. It will take elements from his childhood and adapt them to cooperate with the aims of the retrograde Neptune seeker in the eighth house of adult values. Cancer Neptune gradually grew into an adult faith capable of uniting with the flow of inspiration available at Uranus.

Second Opposition: Retrograde Mars-Saturn-Jupiter

The second opposition is Mars conjunct retrograde Saturn opposition Jupiter. Awareness of it was delayed by the interception of Aries-Libra. This is a particularly deep split because the ruler of Aries is also intercepted, taking the entire being principle deep under the waters of Pisces.

The fifth house placement makes this a part of the conditioned family role. The first house of the conditioned self-image is dominated by the Sun/father who intends that his son's own identity shall be sacrificed on the Christian cross, at the Pisces fifth house cusp. In the time-space where Joshua grew up, the notion of a personal and spiritual identity simply did not exist. His father not only claimed his own calling, he claimed the right to invest his son's life in that calling. Aries intercepted in the fifth house shows that Joshua had his own calling from birth or before.

Intercepted Mars shows that the conditioned male image is taken for granted. In the belief systems of Joshua's childhood *everyone knew* how men should be, what they should do. This description was set in stone and would go unquestioned for years–until the interception opened, allowing the Mercury square to question it. Meanwhile, the pure raw energy of Aries Mars was disciplined by Saturn, who managed and directed it into the places of greatest need. During the early years, that need was survival of the identity.

The only real limit of Aries Saturn is how much self-awareness we hold, but it often manifests as a place where the need to survive supersedes our true nature. In this chart the survival issues are linked to the conditioned role, which is designed to sacrifice the self to its desires. The Saturn-Mars conjunction is sturdy and determined. Even from its unconscious intercepted position, it will hang on for dear life, in the face of others' beliefs. The opposition shows that it hangs on even more tightly in reaction to the unquestioned beliefs that others hold. The more they believe it, the less Joshua believes it.

The fifth house interception probably accused its native of being angry and irresponsible, when the real difficulty came from fear for the survival of its identity. Because Joshua is doubly Sagittarian, his wisest course was to run away from danger. He did run away from home at age fifteen, and then returned several years later, only to leave again.

First Square: Uranus-Mars-Saturn

The square from Uranus to Mars-Saturn threatened to break up the fifth house program, overturning the conditions on how Joshua was expected to act.[10] A Capricorn-Aries square requires that we finish one thing before we start another. Resolving the Uranus-Neptune opposition was necessary before his ability to see beyond the limits of the current definition of humankind could develop. This development was a prerequisite for opening the interception.

Second Square: Saturn-Mars-Neptune

The square from Saturn-Mars to Neptune defines the energy drain represented by fear for the survival of his inner life. Aries-Cancer says that without activation of the Aries Seed, nothing can be born at Cancer. Later in life a guide born of the Uranus-Neptune marriage advised Joshua on financial investments.

Third Square: Jupiter-Neptune

The square from Neptune to Jupiter shows Neptune's threat to dissolve Jupiter concepts about commitment. The Cancer-Libra square shows the tendency for unresolved childhood fears to interfere with marital peace. The interception of Jupiter shows an unconscious belief about marriage that eventually proved untrue when Neptune dissolved its hold on Joshua's life.

---

[10]Advanced students might wish to ponder the fact that Mars rules Saturn, which in turn rules Uranus. It is this subtle energy exchange that will resolve the square.

Fourth Square: Jupiter-Uranus

The square from Jupiter to Uranus shows rebellion against the beliefs of others, a breaking of tradition. None of Joshua's relationships ever took traditional forms because of his complete commitment to a cosmic truth. He had never entirely accepted his father's beliefs, and spent years traveling the country in search of a belief system he could accept. Eventually he created his own from elements of two religions, then went on to expand on that. Born just before Christmas in 1909, he has always been guided by his own star.

Mystic Rectangle
Higher Consciousness 60°-120°

The sextile and trine are communication aspects. Energy/information flows automatically across trines and can be started easily across sextiles. The only hazard in this configuration is that it might function so smoothly in the patterns learned during childhood that we never analyze them for potential. The advantage of the opposition is that it breaks up old habit patterns, energizing the higher or mystic potential of the configuration. Energy is derived from the resistance of the opposition, speeding up the internal computer.

Liz

First Opposition: Retrograde Uranus-Chiron-Venus

Retrograde Uranus opposite Chiron-Venus lies in the value system,[11] showing that some things are valuable only to Liz and other things are valuable to others.[12] The retrograde position of Uranus takes on its higher meaning as knowledge and/or inspiration. Liz has knowledge that she cannot explain, which is her most significant personal asset; but this was not recognized as a value by the adults in her childhood. It stands in opposition to Chiron-Venus in Gemini, with Chiron as a New Kid marker, with Venus/values in Gemini/words. Someone says, "I love you" often, but its value seems questionable to Liz because this person does not value her most important talent (represented by Uranus). It feels like a very conditional kind of love or one divided/Gemini. It suggests, "I love you for this, but not for that" or "I love you when you do as I say." Venus in the eighth always feels like a demand for, or denial of, love, and as though there is a set of conditions on it. The secret of the eighth house and its potential for power lies in the fact that it is really an adult value. Still, from the moment we recognize ourselves as adults, we can claim its power to work magic in our lives.

---

[11]Second-eighth house polarity is the value system.

[12]Parents, family, etc. the adults in her childhood

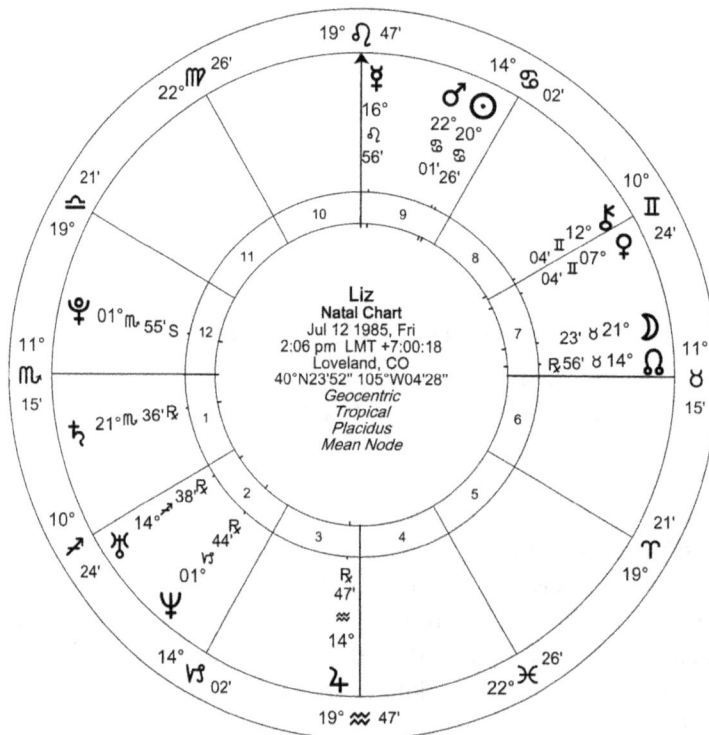

Liz
Natal Chart
Jul 12 1985, Fri
2:06 pm LMT +7:00:18
Loveland, CO
40°N23'52" 105°W04'28"
Geocentric
Tropical
Placidus
Mean Node

I am reminded of a situation that came up in Liz's life around puberty. Liz studied piano (Chiron/hands, Venus/music) and became quite a good pianist. Her father was so proud of the accomplishment that he insisted she perform for every family gathering. Liz soon tired of that, knowing that being a pianist was neither her destiny nor her most important talent. The Uranus-Sun-Mars combo rebelled and she stopped playing altogether.

Perhaps in time Liz will be able to return the music to her life–and maybe even be able to play the *music of the spheres* that she seems to have heard all of her life.

Second Opposition: Mercury-Jupiter

Jupiter represents our capacity for deductive reasoning and can be imaged as the operating system of a computer. We use it to calculate more information from what our Mercury/senses have brought us. In this way it expands our energy/information. When Jupiter is retrograde, the expansion is conditioned by our concept of *enough*. Retrograde Jupiter always brings us *enough*, but that amount depends on how much we believe is enough. Any planet placed in Aquarius functions *between the worlds*[13] and/or at a genius level. Aquarius Jupiter has an extraordinary capacity to

---

[13]That particular part of being functions from a perspective expanded beyond *normal* limits, as defined by world consciousness. It might be called galactic–between Heaven and Earth.

figure out what is going on. Placed in the fourth house, it develops at home, in private. Too much togetherness interferes with the Jupiter function.

This Jupiter really needs space! Placed in opposition to Leo Mercury, at first Liz must choose between the outer voice and the inner one. With Mercury ruling Venus, we know that in the early environment Mercury has the greater capacity for winning approval. It approves of learning, provided that she does not know too much. Again, Jupiter is retrograde so the trick is to recite just enough to get the desired reactions from the family. This opposition sets up a regulator on how much wisdom is allowed to come out of the mouth! The Mystic Rectangle shows potential, i.e., what is available.

Initially, retrograde Uranus often feels frustration. Placed in the second house, the frustration can be used to energize the kind of changes that will get Liz away from home and the overly-tight family bonds. Uranus is sextile Jupiter in the fourth, which allows flow, meaning that her connection lies just beneath the surface of awareness, like a machine *plugged in*, waiting to be turned on.

Closer observation shows that the two are in mutual reception. When they are *turned on* they will function like a conjunction. The result is intuitive wisdom that spreads out concentrically–like ripples from a stone dropped into a pool–to the farthest reaches of the universe.

Venus can only be accurately named after the age of emancipation, when it becomes an adult value. At that point, it becomes the personal value of consciousness–Liz loves information, is a natural seeker,[14] who values learning and loves asking questions. The trine between Jupiter and Venus facilitates the *marriage* required by the Jupiter-Mercury opposition. The love of learning will intensify–and thus empower–the capacity to receive intuitive answers through Uranus' inspiration. This is pictured by the trine between Mercury and Uranus.

The Mystic Rectangle is designed to link the two worlds through the person of Liz. If the reader will compare this chapter with the previous one on the Grand Cross, the mystical function of the chart structure can be pictured. Initially the cross makes life difficult, but those difficulties activate the Mystic Rectangle. Liz is like a highly spiritualized human computer, and like all computers, she runs on resistance. She has chosen this mission because she cares about the survival of the Children of Earth. Although the *web of information* available is huge, there are natural regulators that withhold information until it is asked for, until the time is right. This means that little energy is wasted and the child is not overburdened with information until she matures sufficiently to handle it without undue emotional stress. Puberty is a difficult time because the transition from child to adult is of much greater magnitude than is generally expected. Still, the effort will pay off in time and the rewards will be rich.

---

[14]As confirmed by retrograde Neptune.

Attunement Rectangle
102°-78°

Dividing a 360° circle by seven produces the septile group. These aspects always result in fractions of degrees and are thus difficult to see. The approximate arcs are: septile: 51° 26", bi-septile: 102° 51", and tri-septile: 154° 17". In this example the two oppositions are connected by two bi-septiles and two 3/14 angles (1.5 septile).

Seventh harmonic linkages exist within us like musical chords waiting to be sounded. When the outer planets make transiting aspects to them, they reverberate, sometimes chaotically, leading to creative changes in our lives. Here, we are linked to the invisible realm and must trust in the guidance and assistance that come from there.

Seventh harmonic aspects belong to a higher level of consciousness and being which is just beginning to become apparent on Earth. They are aspects of internal union and impersonal commitment, intended to leave a mark on the world. In the septile, the influence of the seventh sign, Libra, is transformed to that of the inner partner, who shares our joys and sorrows and never abandons us–even when we forget or deny its existence.

Raphael

First Opposition: Libra-Aries

The first opposition is the Libra-Aries horizon, with Neptune conjunct the Ascendant. Libra rising is "The Other." Raphael's otherness was that while his siblings breezed through school with relative ease, for him it was all a struggle. With Neptune rising and opposite the Aries Descendant, there was little assertiveness in him and he spent far too much of his childhood on the sidelines of life.

Diagnosed as *learning disabled*, Raphael was assigned a place in a *special* class, with developmentally disabled children. This was a mixed blessing for a boy who was exceptionally bright but unable to express it.

Raphael was twelve when he finally got an accurate diagnosis: dyslexia. He was given visual training to teach his eyes how to see properly. A few weeks into the training he told his mother, "Mama, I really can read." By midyear he had gained enough self-confidence to go

to bat for himself. He wanted out of the *special* class and he accomplished his goal. Life continued to be more difficult for Raphael than for most people, but he persevered, fighting physical pain and bouts of depression; he continued the struggle and became a significant model for the ability to overcome life difficulties.

Second Opposition: Jupiter-Chiron

The second opposition is Leo Jupiter in the tenth house opposition a retrograde Aquarius Chiron in the fourth. The real difference between direct and retrograde Chiron is choice. Direct Chiron offers the opportunity to choose, but retrograde Chiron makes choice a mandate. Retrograde Chiron often marks a lifetime in which many adjustments are required for survival in the family and circumstances of birth. Certain talents and abilities must be repudiated, put away, ignored, or forgotten because they anger or frighten the adults around us. This assigned his Leo Jupiter–with its conjunction to Uranus–the task of holding onto hope.

Raphael's mother had grown up under a wide variety of abuses but did not realize that her family would treat her son as badly as they had treated her. When she had to be hospitalized at the time of Raphael's first birthday, there seemed no alternative to leaving him with that family. When his parents picked him up a few days later he was a changed little boy. Many years passed before he was able to tell his mother about how he had been treated, after asking a question about something that he had *seen* (psychically). The reaction to his question was so severe that Raphael shut down his entire right brain.[15]

In addition, Chiron's aspects to the remainder of the chart are nearly all negative. An important one is an opposition to Uranus. In his twenties, Raphael joined the Navy and ended up with a severe back injury that went untended until he was able to see a civilian doctor, who validated his injury as a broken vertebra. This resulted in years of pain that Raphael learned to control psychically. In time, employment training changed his life, he married and built a home.

Some years later, he found a way to use his intuitive gifts for others. He and his wife run a School for White Magic, teaching spiritual principles to the young people of their neighborhood. There is magic and power in Raphael's Scorpio Moon-Saturn conjunction in the first house, and the robes of a Mage suit him well.

[15]Raphael struggled mightily through school, diagnosed with a learning disability, which was eventually re-diagnosed as dyslexia. The effect was much the same as occurs when a naturally left-handed child is forced to the right.

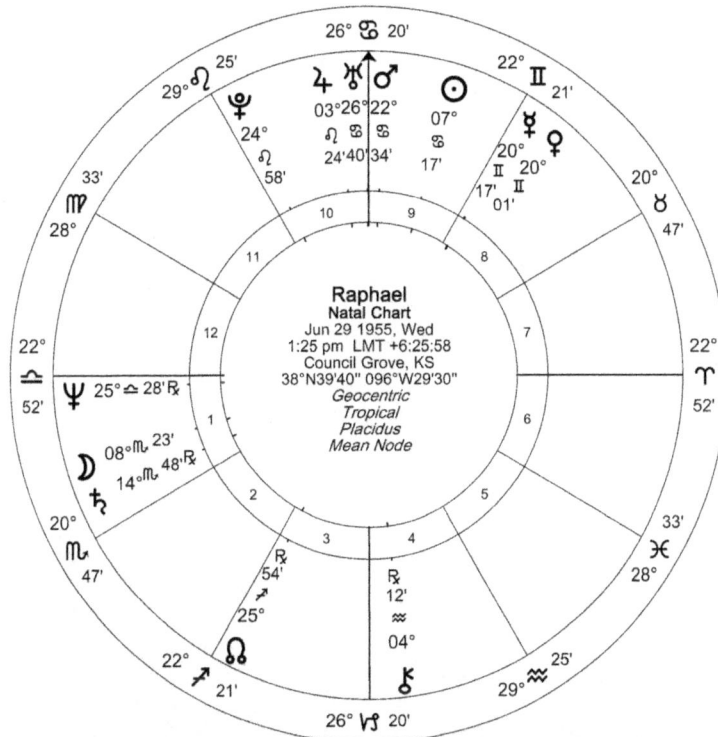

Raphael
Natal Chart
Jun 29 1955, Wed
1:25 pm LMT +6:25:58
Council Grove, KS
38°N39'40" 096°W29'30"
Geocentric
Tropical
Placidus
Mean Node

The Septile Construct: Mercury, Chiron, Jupiter, Neptune

Keep in mind that any Rectangle expresses grounding, so this one speaks of grounded attunement–an expression for being *in the world, but not of the world.*

The human consciousness-structure is comprised of Mercury, Chiron, Jupiter, and Neptune. Three-fourths of this is involved in his seventh harmonic Rectangle. Leo Jupiter is 1.5 septiles (3/14) from the Ascendant-Neptune conjunction. It is, in turn, biseptile to retrograde Chiron, while Mercury conjunct Venus is opposition Neptune.

This consciousness works quite differently from the general population. Raphael is a kind of *thought musician* who puts ideas together the way musical notes are combined to form chords. Mercury-Venus in Gemini may well be considered a *voice.*

At birth he was given the name of an angel, and to some it seems that you can almost see him singing the stars into place. On Earth he has had to struggle as though his wings had been clipped to keep him here. Still, there is a grace in him that allows us to imagine him at the end of his Earth journey on gorgeous widespread wings, soaring back home.

Potential Rectangle
Developing Creativity 36º-144º

The decile (thirty-six degrees) is a semi-quintile and compares with the quintile as the semi-sextile does to the sextile. Creativity is present but requires awareness to start the flow of energy across the decile. The bi-quintile (144 degrees) represents a creative flow with the automatic nature of a trine. Like the trine, it can degenerate to a habit unless it has some resistance to activate its potential. In this configuration, oppositions provide that resistance.

Lisa

First Opposition: Ascendant-Descendant

The Ascendant-Descendant axis splits naturally in our initial programing. The first house describes our instructions about how we are or should be. The seventh house describes our instructions about how we are not or should not be. Additionally, the seventh describes our first other, usually our mother. She becomes the model for our choice of mates later in life. Agreeing with the nature of the decile, it will not become active as the partnership house before puberty, delaying the emergence of the creativity inherent in the decile.

The Ascendant is opposition and the Descendant is conjunct Uranus and retrograde Venus, intensifying the already intense Scorpio-Taurus axis. Around puberty, Venus backed into the Aries interception by secondary progression. At that time Venus effectively *fell through the cracks* of the sixth house so that Lisa's personal values were submerged under work and health issues. This was unusually significant because Venus rules the seventh house. Disappearing just at puberty, it damaged her ability to attract appropriate partners.

The theme was inherent in the Libra interception, which drops relational issues beneath the

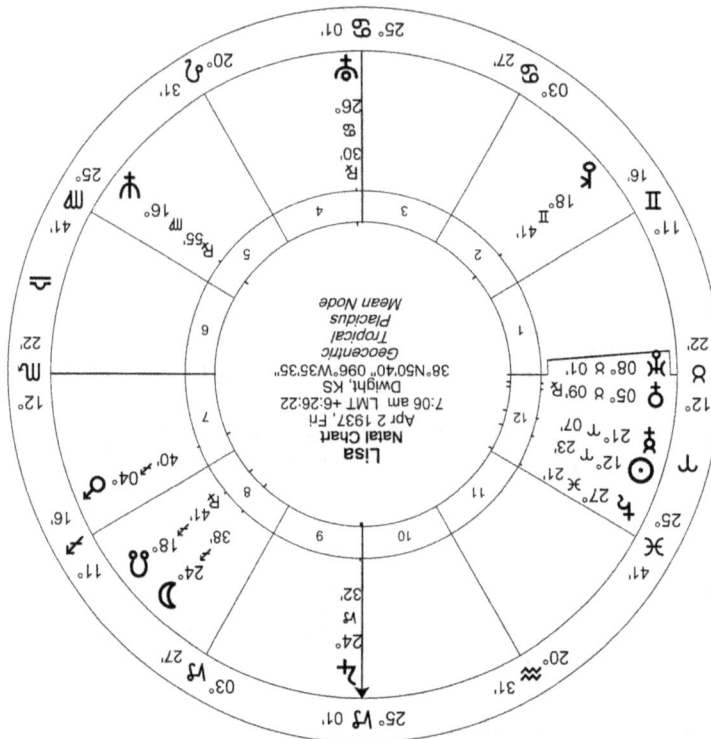

Lisa
Natal Chart
Apr 2 1937, Fri
7:06 am LMT +6:26:22
Dwight, KS
38°N50'40" 096°W35'35"
Geocentric
Tropical
Placidus
Mean Node

subconscious twelfth house. The entire issue of equality was forgotten as though it had never existed. Lisa grew up believing that women do the major part of the work in relationship, so her relationships *proved* her belief. Each husband was in some way irresponsible and undependable. Four marriages and four divorces occurred before she fully grasped that equality was a requirement for partnership.

Second Opposition: Nodal Axis

The Nodal axis initially acts like an opposition. We get attention/energy from others at the North Node, intended to be given to others at the South Node. Implied instructions say that we should pay attention to the South Node but not to the North Node. In the example chart, the outer/house command is to pay attention to how much love and money others have, even to give it to them because they need us. Meanwhile, others pay attention to how much love and money we have and to what we are worth to them. Subtle issues of ownership and control over money and love/sex underlie this area.

The Nodal axis is also the place from which consciousness rises. The Nodes must be seen as a couple. In the naturally occurring state, the input at the North Node is equal to the output at the South, but certain errors in judgment interfere with its flow. If we hold judgments on giving or receiving, we short out our internal energy systems and our chakras become unbalanced.

In this example, the axis is Sagittarius-Gemini, pointing to the personal value of answers being confronted by the dis-value of questions. This naturally forced the forbidden questions into the secret areas of the subconscious, as shown by the eighth house placement of the South Node.

Third Opposition: Chiron-North Node

Treating Chiron as the ruler of Virgo and the natural sixth house, we notice that the physical experience opposes the value of personal beliefs. As the wounded healer, Chiron represents the underground experience of incest, later reflected by sexually abusive mates. The demand for secrecy about the incest blocked her ability to attract love, money, and answers to certain questions.

First Decile: Ascendant-North Node

The first decile is Ascendant to North Node, and by sign the aspect is a semi-sextile, which normally would not communicate. However, the decile aspect turned this into an argument that went on interminably, demanding answers that could not be found in the usual way.

The Scorpio Ascendant is naturally powerful, but when power is ascribed to a child by a parent, it comes as blame. Generosity should bring approval at the North Node. Initially it did so, but when Venus regressed into the interception, parental approval went with it. The Sagittarian North Node will attract answers, even when the questions are forbidden. The chart structure simply drove the questions inside where the depth of Scorpio combined with the breadth of Sagittarius to bring answers from the far reaches of space and time. In this way the frustration of childhood became the motivating force for expanding consciousness in her adult years.

Second Decile: Descendant-Uranus-Venus/South Node-Chiron

The second decile is Descendant-Uranus-Venus to South Node-Chiron. By the time the seventh house evolves to its adult meaning as conscious commitment, its ruler has regressed into the interception and is effectively comatose. This leaves Uranus in power as the ruler of significant others who are different from what the Ascendant calls for. Lisa attracted men who were reacting to her self-image rather than those who reflected it. They valued her (Taurus) not for whom she was but for what she could do for or give to them. Each of them had some part of his life out of control. They expected her to magically "fix" their lives, and she tried.

The Gemini South Node naturally generates questions, ideas, and words. This is the natural speaker and/or writer whose work will question existing ideas. Placed in the eighth house, this is initially forbidden, denied, taboo—especially questions about sex, death, and other eighth house matters. However, Gemini always splits, so some are good and some are not-good. The Chiron conjunction shows that experience taught Lisa how to sort them into proper categories as she learned whom to talk to about what.

The South Node kept asking why Lisa's experience of others--especially significant others--was so erratic. Because the North Node energy was being drained off by her generosity, financial issues prevented the kind of counseling that might have healed her soul wounds.[16] She *accidentally*/Uranus stumbled into the study and practice of astrology, where she has become a pioneer writer in psycho-spiritual astrology.

Bi-quintile: South Node-Ascendant

South Node bi-quintile the Ascendant shows the natural result. Lisa created a double self-image, keeping her true self buried beneath the surface of the Scorpio Ascendant as validated by the intercepted Sun. In the neighborhood where she lives she is known as Granny—the lady who crochets caps for the children and sometimes for their parents. At the same time her work as a *reader* and writer is spreading out from her home office to reach around the world.

---

[16]Negative aspect to the Moon/Soul.

Transformation Rectangle
45°-135°

Eighth harmonic aspects are quadrates, based on a division of the 360 degree circle into eighths. Six of them are included as squares and oppositions. The two remaining are the semi-square (forty-five degrees) and the sesquiquadrate (135 degrees). Traditionally these two have been treated like weakened squares; however, when these aspects are close, quadrates may not feel so weak. Because they are often overlooked, they sometimes trip you up, just when you thought you had gotten past the difficulties they represent.

The semi-square and sesquiquadrate are like dysfunctional Venus energy. The linked planets resemble two magnets turned opposite so they resist each other.

Semi-squares show lack of integrity. The two actors will not combine; like oil and water they do not mix. Sesquiquadrates do not relate. Neither element adequately reflects the other. Unequal, they are incompatible and refuse to cooperate.

Quadrates have an appearance of "that's just the way it is," something that's difficult to overcome. As consciousness rises in the general population, they become self-fulfilling prophecies. By our belief in the judgments, we create their *proof.* Until we resolve them, they cause difficulties in our social relationships (especially marital ones).

Like inconjuncts, the quadrates often represent people in our childhood who created constant tension in the atmosphere. While the inconjuncts will not usually converse at all, the quadrates may argue. They engage in a running battle, with each person determined to win the child over to their point of view. Inconjuncts fight over the child's mind and belief system. Quadrates fight over the child's love and value system.

How these aspects express on a personal level can be assessed from the elements and modes involved. Very often these show issues of self-worth. We may be reacting with dislike due to their (physical or spiritual) resemblance to, or difference from, our own self-image or intentions.

A common misconception is one that suggests that to be truly spiritual you must live celibate and/or in poverty. Another is the idea of the *starving artist*, which requires choosing between developing talents and having financial security. A third is a gender-belief about what is possible or acceptable for males, or for females.

Resolution: Expansion of consciousness is the key. It is one's belief system or value system that must be questioned. In the end, the only power such programmed choices have is the power we give them by our belief.

This Rectangle is between the Midheaven-IC and the nodal axis, with the Aquarius Midheaven semi-square the Capricorn South Node and the Leo foundation (fourth house cusp) semi-square the Cancer North Node.

Sally

First Opposition: Midheaven-IC

With the IC/foundation of the chart in Leo, the chart shows *inherited roots*. There is a family issue over how members of *this family* are or should be. This is in direct opposition to the impersonal Aquarius goal that intends a significantly different goal from that which is planned by the adults in Sally s childhood. She is *going places* neither imagined nor approved by her biological family.

Second Opposition: Nodal Axis

This nodal axis is in a natural position, from Cancer/birth/growth to Capricorn/maturity. Again the nature of the signs points to considerable change over time as Sally matures. The Cancer North Node attracts nurturers.

Sally's Gemini Moon, ruler of the North Node, suggests *two mothers*. She is likely a younger child with an older sister[17] as an assistant nurturer. As a consequence she entrained two different need systems and they argue in her psyche. Because the North Node falls in the second house, this is in some way a personal asset. We note that her Chiron/choice is in Pisces, sign of mastery. At some point after Chiron's discovery in 1977, Sally realized that the true answer for her dilemma was to choose her own very personal need system based on her Taurus Sun. This would take some time, due to the interception of her Sun.

Because it is exempted from the twelfth house by the interception, it will manifest in the sixth. In time, work or health issues will make her true needs obvious.

With the South Node in Capricorn, the spiritual goal is maturation. Because it is in the eighth house, that maturation will be criticized or objected to by the adults in her childhood. Sally may

---

[17]See Venus conjunct her Cancer North Node.

Sally
Natal Chart
May 13 1964, Wed
5:53 am LMT +5:05:09
Norfolk, VA
36°N50'48" 076°W17'08"
Geocentric
Tropical
Placidus
Mean Node

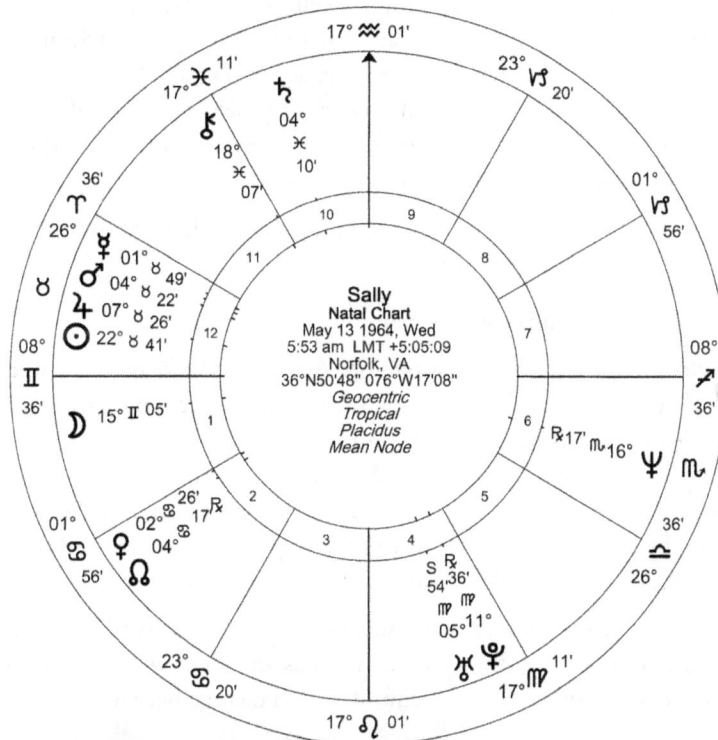

thus emancipate herself before those adults are ready because she knows *instinctively* that her ultimate goal in life is an impersonal one (Aquarius Midheaven) that she needs room to grow into it.

First Semi-Square: North Node-IC

The North Node is semi-square the IC, suggesting that her roots are seemingly somewhat misplaced. She does not really *fit* into her family, and because of that the Sun interception hides much of her light during her early years. She knows that what she came to do has value, but until she is able to find her own place in life she cannot discover what that is or how her world really works.

It can be noted that her Mercury-Mars-Jupiter conjunction will give her more *push* and *enthusiasm* than is normally expected of Taurus–but then she is a new type of Taurus.[18]

Second Semi-Square: South Node-Mars

The South Node describes something to which we are designed to *pay attention*. Here is where the attention/energy given us at the North Node is intended to be invested. As noted, the Capricorn South Node is in the eighth house, which early in life is forbidden or denied to the child.

---

[18]The interception makes her more truly a Taurus-Scorpio for, in her, the two signs are fused from birth, although she may not notice it until her forties or fifties.

Interestingly enough, all attention is energy, so even *negative* attention can be used to *drive* us to the South Node goal. By aspect, Sally's Mars functions like a conjunction and it is trine her Virgo Uranus. This suggests a bit of rebellion that can serve her well. She may one day realize that she can thank family members who resisted her *for driving her to become who she is.* Her ultimate (Aquarius) goal is to become a type of priestess. Her most important hopes and wishes are directed to the nurture of growth and maturation of humanity-as-a-whole.

Coming into this incarnation, Sally brought the tools she would need to confront and overcome family resistance to her spiritual commitments.

First Sesquiquadrate: North Node-Midheaven

Sally's Cancer North Node is sesquiquadrate her Aquarius Midheaven. Viewed traditionally as Cancer/nurture and Aquarius/detachment, they seemed completely incompatible. However, taking a different point of view showed a more positive potential. The two sign rulers, Moon and Uranus, have one thing in common: both are about change. Cancer reflects ordinary short-cycle changes that happen daily, monthly, yearly. Aquarius reflects more unusual, long-cycle changes such as are described by the aspects of Uranus to its own place. Together they will present her with a series of small changes that accumulate into some very large changes.

This will be based on the way that consciousness works. Even the weakest of ideas, called hopes and wishes, when compounded over time will manifest as *dreams come true* when their time is right. All of the little changes compounded will accumulate and change her whole life.

Second Sesquiquadrate: IC-North Node

The Leo foundation is sesquiquadrate the Capricorn North Node. This suggests that Sally's real heritage is not so much a physical one as a spiritual one. Leo is ruled by that hidden Sun, which hides her light until she is old enough and big enough for it to shine safely in all its mature/Capricorn glory. Here it is clear that the child is the parent and precursor of the adult. Leo will shine, albeit not in the same way as her ancestors. Unlike them, she comes from the future, not the past.

In the final analysis the meridian shows that Sally is a Light Bearer. During her early years–for the sake of preserving her life and/or identity–her light was kept *turned down.*

However, by the grace of that wonderful hidden Taurus stellium, the day would come when a transit–most likely by Uranus–would switch it on and flood her environment with light. Even as she *lights up lives*, she also enlightens them by her presence and/or her good works.

Gestation Rectangle
Multiples of the Novile

Ninth harmonic aspects are called noviles (sometimes called nonagens or noniles). In the series we find the novile (forty degrees), the bi-novile (eighty degrees), and the quarto-novile (160 degrees). We also see semi-noviles (twenty degrees) and 140 degree combinations. These should be allowed no more than one to one and a half degrees of orb.

Forty is a number often used symbolically in Judeo-Christian scripture; specifically, the journey through the wilderness to the Promised Land in the old testament and Jesus' forty days in the wilderness after his baptism. These image the period of *feeling lost* that follows each time our consciousness shifts to the next level.

Perhaps more relevant to today's readers is the forty-week human gestation period. During that period life begins *in the dark of the womb*, remaining there until its time of deliverance, until it is ready to emerge into the light.

Of the nine traditional planets, Pluto is the ninth. (Pluto's best known meaning is that of metamorphosis, symbolized by the butterfly, whose rebirth occurs in the dark of a cocoon and is later delivered into the light.) Combining the numbers from being the ninth part of the circle and its forty-degree length, noviles are symbolic of periods when new life is gestating unseen, sometimes quite slowly, until its proper time to emerge, to be born or reborn.

Because most noviles require time to unfold, people sometimes believe that their gifts must be earned. While this is a common element in various belief systems, it is never true (any more true than that an infant or a butterfly) that it can be made to earn its way into the light. These processes are ordained by Deity, or by Nature, and much as we sometimes find it irritating, we have no control over them. The only solution is to let go of our conditioning around them, irrevocably and permanently. We are required to give up, accepting defeat, and wait for their time of fulfillment.

Only then can noviles be transformed–as by metamorphosis. Releasing all conditioning around the planetary relationship, we must reinterpret them at the sign (or archetypal) level. The measure of their dysfunction relative to the houses is the measure of their efficiency when released from the realm of conditioned response. When applied to our incarnational purpose they become true power points, sometimes dancing for joy!

Noviles may show an incarnation committed to raising consciousness in Self and/or Others. That commitment forces ritualistic behavior designed to rewrite our early conditioning. This may then permit mysterious and/or magical revelations. New elements of power enter Earth, fostered by a type of procreative process at the nonphysical level.

We might also notice that the ninth sign is Sagittarius, which can signify escape, abandonment, freedom, and/or enlightenment. Escaping the belief systems of the past, we discover *new and greater truths*. Abandoning the old, we receive the new. Giving up *safe limits*, we move beyond them to higher ground. Always there is some element of passing through desolation to discover that which sets us free. Literally, this is an aspect of overcoming, where we rise up over the obstacles created by the mind of man.

Wholly impersonal, ninths are active only in those committed to the good of the whole. Activity around it is out of our conscious control, mandated by the master-plan to which we are committed and the resistance in the general consciousness which surrounds us.

Terri

Terri's Rectangle is comprised of her Gemini-Sagittarius horizon and her Virgo-Pisces Nodal Axis. She is a New Kid, with a common Indigo signature: Mars in Aries. Clearly she will need it, with Saturn conjunct Uranus–broken boundaries–confronting her Gemini Ascendant. She also has Chiron–the signature of upgraded humanity represented by the New Kids–as her rising planet. Still, with her chart *hung on* a ninth harmonic Rectangle, it will take time for her to discover who, what, and why she came to Earth at this time, and through that particular family.

First Opposition: The Horizon

Although her traditional Ascendant is Gemini, as a New Kid her self-image is more truly Gemini-Sagittarius. Ultimately this is the signature of a messenger–one who learns/Gemini in order to teach/Sagittarius in order to learn in order to teach . . . and so on. This horizon is about a lifelong rise in consciousness.

However, with the opposition to that retrograde Saturn-Uranus conjunction, on the descending side of the chart she begins life with Gemini/questions about the Sagittarius/beliefs held by her family. Her Leo Sun in the third house side of the conditioned belief system[19], there is an expecta-

---

[19]Third-ninth axis.

07° ♓ 55'

11° ♈ 17'

10° ♒ 21'

♂
11°
♈
11'

14°
♓
52'
℞

20'
♉
18°

04° ♊ 08'
♃

16°
♑
33'

23°
♊
17'

Terri
Natal Chart
Aug 20 1988, Sat
0:43 am LMT +6:29:35
Corpus Christi, TX
27°N48'01" 097°W23'46"
Geocentric
Tropical
Placidus
Mean Node

℞38' ♑07' ♆

℞09' ♐27' ♅

℞00' ♐26' ♄

23°
♐
17'

05° ♋ 05'
⚷

11° ♋ 44'
♀

16°
♋
33'

14' ♏23'

02' ♏10'
♇
18°

♓
20'

29'
♌
27'

28'
♍
13'

11° ♎
17'

10° ♌ 21'

☉

☿

07° ♍ 55'

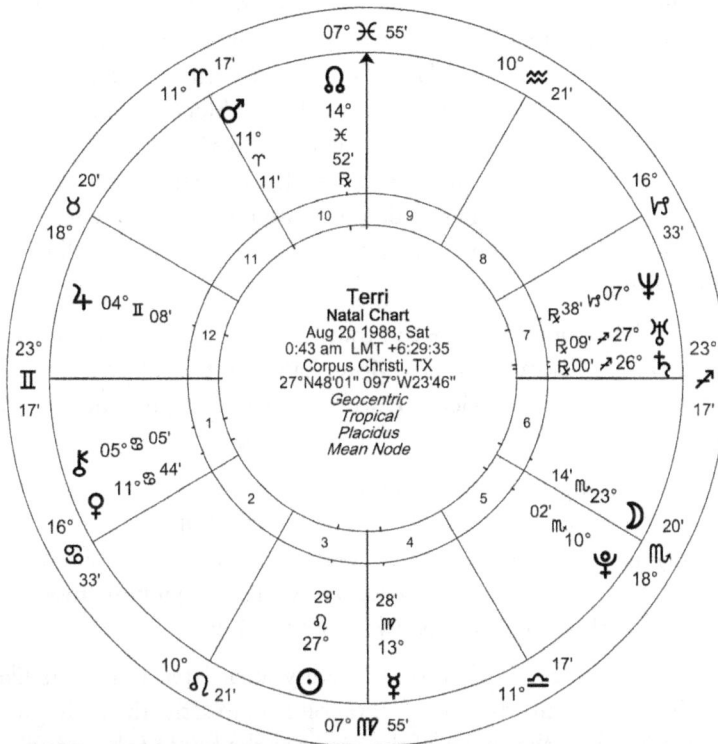

tion of or command to think like the family, to hold to the family beliefs. Still, the Scorpio Moon–linked to Pluto–does not easily take orders. Terri *sees through* what is essentially a *rote religion* and those who memorize it without looking for meaning. One can almost hear that Gemini Ascendant asking, "How can they believe that? Why do they believe that?"

The power behind that questioning actually comes from that Sagittarius conjunction, which is also conjunct the Galactic Center.

Terri is linked to the *Sun behind the Sun* in a way that amounts to a direct link to the Galactic or Universal Mind. It may take her time (Ninth Harmonic) to *figure out* how to fit all the pieces together, but with the help of rising Chiron there is little doubt that she will do so. At that point she will realize that the family belief system really does not make sense.

Second Opposition: Nodal Axis

The North Node in Pisces in the tenth house conjunct the Midheaven is opposition the South Node in Virgo conjunct Mercury and the IC. Viewed as conditioning, this is a command that *you cannot get there from here.* Technically the meridian goes one way and the nodal axis goes the other. Only a New Kid would instinctively realize that every goal is inherent in its *starting gate.*

The overall structure of this chart suggests that Terri was born left-handed and thus right brained, but that the adults in her childhood forced her to use the right hand. In doing so they may have caused problems that would be labeled as *learning disabilities*. This practice was officially intended to help *lefties* fit into a right-dominant world. More subtly, it blocked, or at least hindered, the development of natural right-brained, intuitive dominance. If this happened it could be easy to blame those adults for the unusually long time it takes for full development of self-awareness and spiritual potential. More accurately, it allowed her to demonstrate means of overcoming the dyslexia that it almost certainly caused. For the highly evolved there is a kind of gift in all of this. Eventually it teaches whole-brain thinking.

Returning to the vertical opposition, we can translate this same energy into the realization that Virgo's practice ever leads to Piscean Mastery. More than that, the subtle effect of having both the foundation of the chart in Virgo and Mercury, with the nodal output, and the South Node[20] also in Virgo, tends to subtly shift the life into the present moment.

While it is not entirely clear how that works at this time, it reminds me of the *calling* of intercepted Sun people. While most interceptions mark Possibility People who are here to help with the transition of humanity up to the next (Aquarian) level of consciousness, the intercepted Sun people are here to teach and assist the Possibility People. Many PPs are symbolic monks and nuns, while the intercepted Sun marks their *Mother Superiors* or *Father Abbots*.

Although it may not manifest until Terri's fortieth year or later, it appears likely that she is a designated *New Kid's New Kid*, an advanced generation here to assist the main group of New Kids. Eventual rebirth takes her from the center of the group to the head of the group.

First Semi-novile Construct (5/18): Mercury-South Node/Descendant-Saturn-Uranus

Virgo Mercury-South Node is sesqui-novile the Sagittarius Descendant-Saturn-Uranus. The signs involved are square, and that square will gradually, in time, be overcome by the planets involved. Virgo square Sagittarius puts the body at odds with the spirit. It keeps the native so busy doing his or her *duty*, and/or providing for the physical needs of self or others that there is no time for the spiritual feeding required by Sagittarius. Some Sagittarius/teaching will still take place, but what is taught is the lifestyle. The individual realization needed is that a balance between the physical and spiritual aspects of life is required for health–all kinds of health–as physical, mental, emotional, financial, relational, etc. Much of what we do through sheer physical strength and endurance would be better, and far more easily accomplished, through some type of spiritual practice.

The angle of Mercury-South Node to Saturn-Uranus points to a developmental or gestation process. Their sesqui-novile relationship pictures a long period of slow unfoldment, which leads to a birth or rebirth, an emergence, into the light.

---

[20]North Node in Pisces gets attention/energy from Piscean Masters. In turn, the South Node in Virgo asks that it be invested in Chelas/novitiates.

Virgo Mercury is nothing if not orderly and organized. It is also almost obsessively logical. Retrograde Saturn is empathic. Taken alone, these will keep Terri struggling, trying to choose between what she *sees* and what she *senses*. For some years that struggle will take up the time, energy, and attention that is designated for service by the Virgo South Node.

With Uranus retrograde, Terri must learn to tolerate frustration before she can achieve peace of mind. She may be so certain that she *knows* how to create change that she will accept no help from others. Intuitively knowing that she can do this alone, believing that she should, or simply wanting to prove something, she may stand in her own way.

However, current rising levels of awareness, a gift of her New Kid status, are providing new help for dealing with retrograde Uranus. With patience, affirmations, visualizations, and rituals for creating change will work, but they may take more time than when used by direct Uranus. But then, for the most part, the changes she wishes to make are neither small nor personal ones. This is shown by the conjunction of her Saturn-Uranus to the Galactic Center. Still, that same conjunction will provide a massive power source when the time is right for the changes she envisions.

Second Semi-novile Construct: North Node-Ascendant

Terri's Pisces North Node is sesqui-novile her Gemini Ascendant. The signs are square and that square will gradually be resolved by the sesqui-novile aspect of the two points.

Pisces square Gemini refers to a lack of faith/trust in our ability to learn.[21] If the information received is vague, undefined or contradictory, there can be little growth in consciousness.

A conscious Piscean[22] master would spontaneously overcome these difficulties, but as of this writing very few individuals are able to accept their own mastery, having been taught that mastery cannot be achieved while in a physical body.

Without recognition of her mastery, much of Terri's mind will be smothered/drowned for some years. The result looked like a learning disabled child or one who survived largely on *animal instincts*. Without undue stress she may adapt quite well to using the intuitive mind as a perceptive function. She is, after all, a New Kid, with abilities rarely seen in individuals born before 1968.

That Piscean North Node will attract other Masters to her. From time to time one of these will *see* and recognize her. Gradually the evidence will accumulate and Terri will begin to realize who and what she most truly is. The Leo Sun refers to one who is Daughter of Deity and its brilliant light is channeled through her Scorpio Moon/Soul, giving her magical and miraculous powers. Once she knows her potential, it will begin to unfold. That is, after all, both the personal and the spiritual goal of her life.

Because it takes a long time for her abilities to unfold, Terri will likely be very long-lived. Hav-

---

[21]Another indication of probable dyslexia. Although this creates major learning problems in childhood, many people overcome most of them at or after age thirty.

[22]One who knows herself to be a master–and has not been talked out of it by her elders.

ing finally realized why she incarnated at this time, she will want to stay. This writer believes that her wish to do so will be granted.

Consciousness Rectangle
30°-150°

This Rectangle connects two oppositions, with two pairs of inconjuncts. Inconjuncts are twelfth harmonic aspects. All but two of them are included in other aspect families. The remaining 1/12 and 5/12 angles are called the semi-sextile and the quincunx. The meaning of the two aspects is quite similar.

Inconjuncts involve a mismatching of element and mode. They are in signs that cannot easily communicate with each other through the logical process. They force consciousness-expansion rather compulsively by pitting the body and/or its feelings against the spirit and/or its intelligence Inconjuncts simply refuse to be ignored, coming up time after time until we discover that doing things the same old way always produces the same old results. The only way to get any peace is to find new methods of approach, new ways of doing things.

Inconjuncts represent a *missed connection* between two principles of being. They represent a schematic problem that resembles a short in our wiring. This interferes with communication/semi-sextile or cooperation/quincunx. They will not say what

> **Common Interests in Semi-sextiles**
> - Aries energizes Taurus' structural integrity.
> - Taurus contributes substance to Gemini's ideas.
> - Gemini communicates what Cancer feels.
> - Cancer nurtures Leo's creativity.
> - Leo activates Virgo's mission.
> - Virgo streamlines Libra's designs.
> - Libra reflects Scorpio's power.
> - Scorpio deepens Sagittarian understanding.
> - Sagittarius expands Capricorn's goals, loosening boundaries.
> - Capricorn is the base for Aquarian exploration.
> - Aquarius provides detachment for Piscean visions.
> - Pisces is the whole from which Aries individuality emerges.

they want or need from each other. Each seems to think that the other should know and is too proud to ask. In so doing they interrupt self realization and spiritual growth.

An important approach to resolution of these aspects is to find the commonalities of the signs involved. See the examples given.

Semi-sextiles are sometimes interpreted as mild sextiles, but while sextiles cooperate easily, semi-sextiles have to find some common ground before they can join forces.

Caught between the opposition and the trine, the quincunx often begins life with oppositional difficulties and concludes with the peace of a trine.

> **Common Interests of Quinunxes**
> - Aries-Scorpio both deal in energy/power.
> - Aries-Virgo is pure potential. Aries, being newly emerged, is uncontaminated; Virgo is purified through the realization that she or he is nothing but what she was born to be.
> - Taurus-Sagittarius is natural. Taurus-Libra is love.
> - Gemini-Capricorn is definition/names. Gemini-Libra is relationship.
> - Cancer-Sagittarius is understanding. Cancer-Aquarius is change (internal or external).
> - Leo-Capricorn is presence. Leo-Pisces is unreality.
> - Virgo-Aquarius reminds us that to experience–to be conscious of–is to know.
> - Libra-Pisces: Libra is union with one, Pisces is unity with all.
> - Scorpio-Gemini is magic–the magic of knowing the name.

Bobby

First Opposition: IC-Meridian

The Capricorn IC opposition the Cancer Midheaven pictures life beginning with Capricorn maturity and logic, and asks, "How can I become younger/Cancer?" Or, "Where is there to go from here?" The only way that this axis can really work is with a belief system that includes reincarnational evolution. In a sense this is what the entire chart represents.

The Capricorn foundation sign is the mark of the *Old Soul*, and his reach for the Midheaven is a reach for continuing personal and spiritual growth. When Cancer is at the Midheaven, *the path is the goal.*

Second Opposition: Nodal Axis

Traditionally, the eighth is a house of transformation. It must be that because first it is the *not-mine* house of the child. It contains all the things forbidden children (sex and the occult) or simply not their domain (taxes, investments, insurance, etc.) and includes any special family taboos.

The transformation that occurs is that when we reach adulthood all those same things are ours to claim or own. In time, it will come to mean investments or jointly owned or shared income and/ or property. At its highest level, in the eighth house we may be *invested with power.*

Meanwhile, the second house is our personal assets, the abilities, talents, and valuable/saleable

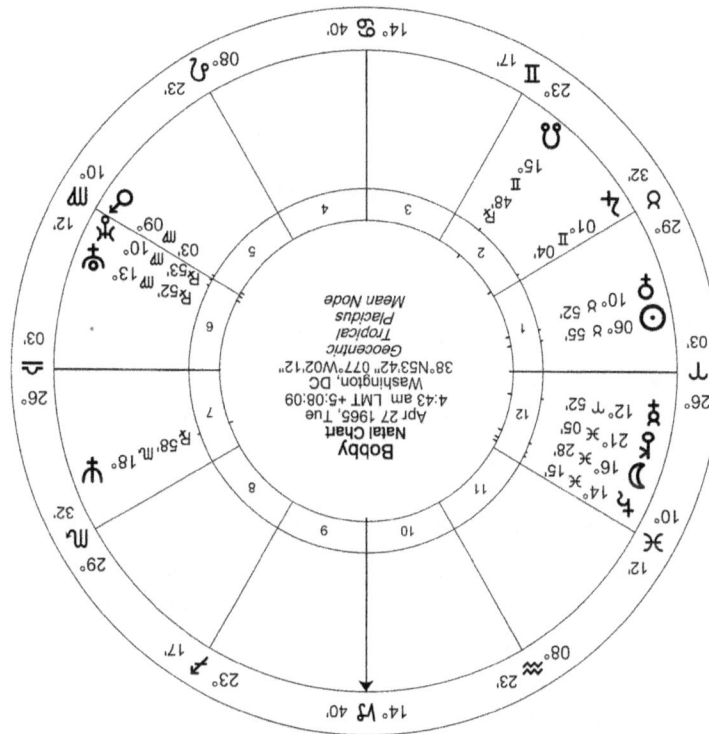

characteristics that we bring into this life at birth. In time, it will come to mean *personal income and property*.

With the Gemini North Node in the eighth house, the child is likely to get much negative attention in the form of criticism or condemnation. Being Gemini, think verbal abuse.

With the Sagittarius South Node, a personal asset is wisdom. He has teaching or counseling ability. Essentially a messenger, he may become a writer, publisher, or broadcaster.

Special Note: Aries Mercury is square the meridian from the sixth-twelfth house axis of consciousness[23] occupation. Meanwhile, the Saturn-Moon conjunction in the sixth house is square the nodal axis. These chart factors will help the adult Bobby to *marry* his oppositions, and *get them truly conversing*.

Upper Semi-Sextile: North Node-Midheaven

The semi-sextile (thirty degrees) is like a malfunction of the Gemini side of Mercury. A sextile

---

[23]The sixth house is visible, hands-on. The twelfth is invisible (forgotten) areas of consciousness that naturally express in dreams and visions. The twelfth can be accessed through various applications of hypnosis, meditation, or divination.

Designs for a New Age

is communication. Half a sextile is two people talking but each is unable or unwilling to listen to the other. They talk *at* each other, but not *to* each other. It may look like communication but there is no transfer of information because both talk and neither listens.

Another version of this is the idea without a *name*. It will represent knowledge you have that cannot be communicated because there is no common *language*. It is nearly impossible to express anything beyond very basic ideas to another whose language is different from yours. You can get your basic needs met, but you cannot discuss religion, philosophy, advanced mathematics, or other abstractions. No *meeting of the minds* can occur. Ideas *slide by* each other without really touching.

The goal of this chart (Midheaven) is personal growth. Meanwhile, the attention received is largely at a *primary* or *elementary* level. To the extent that this refers to education, school may be quite boring for young Bobby. Given the Pisces Moon-Saturn, he may appear to be daydreaming in class, and his teachers may complain that he does not pay attention.

Lower Semi-Sextile: South Node-IC

The Sagittarius South Node in the second house is semi-sextile the Capricorn IC.

A lonely, unloved little boy, Bobby seems to have spent considerable time and effort trying to *figure out* what was *wrong* about him. As a teen, he was *born again*. This ritual for clearing guilt was the first step toward the healing of his sixth house Soul Wounds. His Aries Mercury mind could reclaim its innocence and perhaps emerge from a depression.[24]

With the depression clearing, his native wisdom began to emerge. Notice that the ruler of the South Node is in Gemini, along with the North Node. This augers well for the eventual development of whole-brain thinking.

First Quincunx: North Node-IC

This quincunx (150 degrees) between the Gemini North Node and the Capricorn IC is like the dysfunctional Virgo side of Mercury. It indicates problems handling life situations.

At the ego level, the quincunx represents dysfunctional relationships. This is the place where we cannot make peace with someone or some aspect of self because of a situation or environmental context. Traditional thinking says that we must *forgive and forget*, but the quincunx does not go away so easily. Someone or something will not cooperate with the process of making amends.

Quincunxes often require us to learn how to defer gratification without giving up on our hopes and dreams. This method requires that we set an end-date goal so that we do not keep pushing gratification out into a tomorrow that never comes.

In time the Gemini North Node will attract children/students, and Bobby will be a *wise grand-father to them* even if they are not biologically related. Children-in-consciousness seek out their

---

[24]Saturn in the sixth.

Elders, even as physical children gather at their grandparents' knees.

And because they do, Bobby will become a teacher to many, whether or not he had planned to do so. One of the great gifts of the qunicunx is that, even if we aren't looking, life or Deity simply edges into place. And then, if we scan back across the years, we can see an *educational plan* that has been preparing us from the beginning.

Second Quincunx: South Node-IC

The Sagittarius South Node in the second house is quincunx the Cancer IC. This is a picture of how innate wisdom continues to spread outward in concentric rings. Bobby really is a messenger, bringing each person what he or she most needs. In this way he ever nurtures the growth of wisdom in this world and in its inhabitants.

Part II

Yod Configurations

Introduction

The Yod aspect pattern is a configuration between at least three planets or points in the horoscope that creates a long triangle that looks like a witch's hat. Each Yod *has the feel of a fated* aspect pattern, denoting a special mission or destiny in life. Yods have been called the Finger of Fate, Finger of God, and the Projection Triangle, and have been the source of much debate and controversy within the astrological community.

The name of the Yod comes from the tenth Hebrew letter, which has significant cabalistic and mystical significance regarding the name of God, God's omnipresence, and our humility. Its pattern creates a particular and strong energy, stronger than you would get by these aspects on their own.

Like a crystal, each Yod has a very definite and unique structure that holds a special kind of energy. At its most positive the energy of the two base planets is focused like a laser beam on the activation point, directly opposite the fulcrum, or foot, of the Yod. For most traditionalists, the only valid Yod is the standard one with two points in sextile and a third quincunx both. A few modern astrologers also use the golden Yod, with two points quintile and a third bi-quintile both. Six kinds of Yods are discussed in this book.

Any Yod is a relatively uncommon configuration in the shape of an isosceles triangle. The sum of the three angles must be 360 degrees. My personal preference is to keep the combined orb of variation for the three angles to no more than five degrees. Each Yod is comprised of a base fulcrum and an activation point.

The Yod is a tricky but very rewarding formation to study because it offers so much potential insight for self-discovery and learning. Complex and difficult to delineate, they are well worth the effort. Each is a problem with a gift in its hands. It is the highest honor to assist the Yod bearer in his or her life journey and voyage of self-discovery.

Because I believe that we choose our incarnations, I feel that every Yod indicates a preincarnational promise or commitment, rather than being traditionally *destined*. It is as though you made a vow: "I will do this, even if it kills me!"

Yods will not be ignored, tending to repeatedly bring up the same kind of experience until we figure out how to turn their negatives into positives.

While the feeling of *destiny* or *commitment* is common to all Yods, those based on different aspect harmonics have a somewhat different *tone* and/or *color*. Still, any Yod in a natal chart signifies that this is the lifetime in which to bring all of the Yod components together. A kind of gift or talent links the fulcrum planets. The skills are shown by the fulcrum, the challenges by the matching sides, and the mission or task through the apex planet. Although varying in intensity, based on the specific aspect-groups, early in life each activation point represents a conditioned belief or habit that initially resists the gift. That resistance may be guilt, depression, or fear. Whatever the source of resistance, it must be overcome.

Always, certain skills are to be perfected and used in a constructive way to benefit self and others. It is your gift or *special purpose*, your *mission* or *calling*. And it will call to you, shouting if necessary, until you focus your attention on it and begin the work of fulfilling its promise. Rare indeed is the individual who manages to get out of this life without doing so.

Common Interests of Quincunxes

- Aries-Scorpio: both deal in energy/power.
- Aries-Virgo is pure potential. Aries, newly emerged, is uncontaminated; Virgo
- is purified through the realization that she is nothing but what she was born to be.
- Taurus-Sagittarius is natural.
- Taurus-Libra is love.
- Gemini-Capricorn is definition/names.
- Gemini-Scorpio is relationship.
- Cancer-Sagittarius is understanding.
- Cancer-Aquarius is changes (internal or external).
- Leo-Capricorn is presence.
- Leo-Pisces is unreality.

Mindspin

- **First**, acknowledge that although your parent did the best that she or he could, that parenting was not good for you. Tell the truth. You were wounded and you have scars.
- **Do not** try to stop the mind spin in traditional ways. Do not scold or criticize yourself.
- **Acknowledge** that this inner criticism is just an abuse symptom. Be gentle. Learn to laugh at yourself. Say something like, "There I go again," and say it with a rueful chuckle.
- **Instead,** distract yourself whenever you notice that you are in mindspin. Do something that will engage your mind elsewhere. Some people read romances or watch sit-coms or soap operas. Some use exercise. It does not matter what you use, as long as it makes your inner critic shut up.
- **No fair criticizing yourself for the time it takes to do this exercise!**

The Original, or Standard, Yod
Sextile, Quincunx, Quincunx

This Yod is a twelfth harmonic construct. The two quincunxes (also called the inconjunct) are five-twelfths each. The sextile is two-twelfths or one-sixth.

At 150 degrees, the quincunx is one sign short of an opposition, and one sign past a trine. Being thirty degrees short of an opposition and thirty degrees too long to be a trine, the energy here doesn't quite know what to do with itself and can result in the subject feeling out of control from time to time.

A significant key to resolving any quincunx problem is to discover the common interests of the signs involved. Very often the problem of the quincunx is that your conditioning is conflicting with your *special purpose*. Those conflicts produce guilt, anger, or fear. These must be resolved, largely through realizing that what your parents taught might well have been proper, efficient, and/or moral for them; you, however, live in a different time and usually at a higher evolutionary level.

Alternatively or alternately, it feels like things are beyond the subject's control. The quincunx is a quirky, awkward aspect that uses a lot of energy. All that energy has nowhere to go if there are no meaningful aspects to any other celestial points. The Finger of God gives all that energy a purpose, a "place to go." If there is an aspect especially apt to cause *mind-spin*, it is the quincunx.

A (traditional) Yod is formed when one planet is quincunx two other planets that are sextile each other. This construct is essentially attention-getting, and attention leads to a rise in consciousness. Because Yods are nearly impossible to ignore, the notion of fate and/or a special life purpose are suggested.

A common challenge for natives in resolving a Yod is that we have learned a belief system that calls us to *higher ground*, while leaving us with feet stuck in the mud of everyday reality. Sometimes it takes many years to realize that whoever or whatever calls us also has the power to free us, if we will stop struggling so hard to do it ourselves.

In some cases the subject may not ever figure out what this purpose is and fulfill it unbeknownst to herself or himself! This is part of the experience of having a special purpose.

Lana

This Yod is particularly interesting in that it is comprised of three retrograde planets, the only retrogrades in the chart. Although classically Yods keep you working on them for a number of years in the current lifetime, this one seems to be continuing from a previous to a present incarnation.

Notice that the Yod point is her foundation planet. The fourth house cusp and the planet closest to it are noted for the ability to symbolize the reason for the current incarnation.

This Yod suggests a continuing study, possibly to handle the situation better this time, or perhaps simply to improve technique or move the whole process to a *higher level.*

Retrogrades: Cancer Uranus, Taurus Jupiter and Sagittarius Mercury[25]

Retrograde Uranus has a greater-than-average *knowledge* of the dynamics of change. These people know how to change themselves and their world. However, this knowledge is nameless and wordless because it is not present in the general consciousness, being considered impossible by family, friends, and acquaintances.

We are frustrated by the seeming lack of change in our lives and we look for something more drastic or visible, but all we see are natural, instinctual, growth processes. It is as though we have lost or forgotten something critical. We feel that life is underpowered, or in some way not right, but initially we cannot find the *missing piece* we need to change it. We may become afraid to wish for too much change because things may get worse instead of better.

It can *feel like/Cancer,* that we have in past lives been a revolutionary. We sense the ability to create large and sweeping changes in life. In some cases these changes have seemed to *cost too much* in personal terms. In other cases, there were dire consequences, such as execution. Always, at some point before leaving that incarnation, there was a wish for a different lifestyle. Even so, there was knowledge—sometimes unconscious—that life is a choice and leadership is a choice. We are never compelled to accept leadership. Retrograde Uranus has made the choice and regretted it. She may be hesitant about making changes again.

---

[25]I believe that any retrograde planet has returned to the same sign it experienced in one or more previous lifetimes. This is not always about a failed grade. It can also be about deeper study, or simply a retrieval of a well developed skill, for use in a particular current project. In any event, this being at least the second journey through the sign, the planet will have some knowledge at birth, so it will be somewhat ahead of the same planet when direct. I like to think of direct planets as having a rating of A, B, C etc, while retrogrades are A+, B+ or C+.

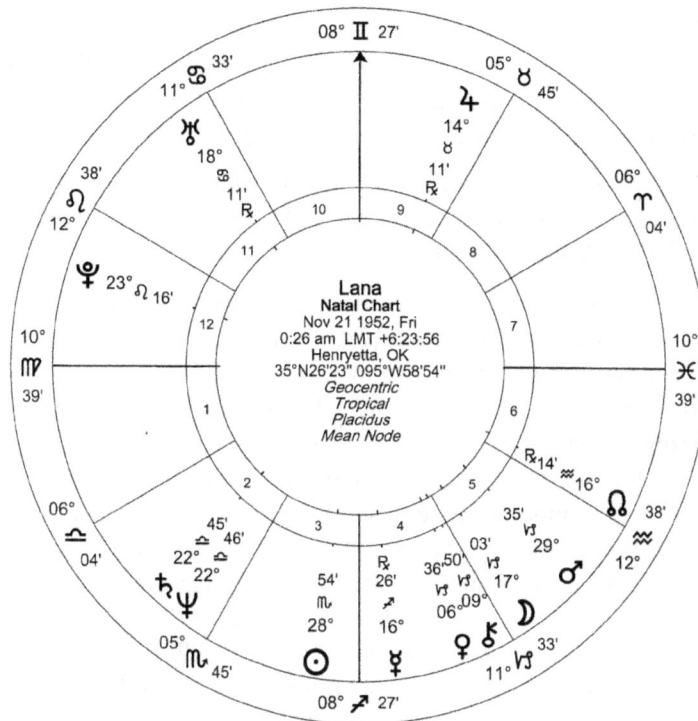

Lana
Natal Chart
Nov 21 1952, Fri
0:26 am LMT +6:23:56
Henryetta, OK
35°N26'23" 095°W58'54"
Geocentric
Tropical
Placidus
Mean Node

With natal Jupiter retrograde, we must discover and live by our own truth because the belief systems of the adults in our childhood simply will not work for us. We may try to make sense of them, but we cannot. In time we realize that they really did not make sense, at least for us. Formally or informally, many study comparative religion, as they piece together their own very necessary personal belief system.

Conditioned beliefs will not work for us because they belong to a younger level of consciousness. It is not profitable for individuals who know calculus to count on their fingers, and it will not work very well.

Jupiter retrograde always signifies a relatively high level of wisdom[26] which is the product of an advanced ability to conceptualize. These individuals are capable of, and must use, this ability. The only valid belief system for them will be one which they assemble for themselves.

Retrograde Jupiter offers the opportunity to live without fear in the knowledge that all needs will be met as they become needs. This is particularly true when it is placed in Taurus. When we commit fully to the spiritual path, we can leave our physical needs in the hands of a Greater Power, trusting the supply.

[26]Within the context of the sign.

Designs for a New Age

This is an effect of an internal understanding that all needs are supplied by God, or by the nature and principle of life. Life abhors a vacuum and will thus fill it. As we learn to trust God or trust the principle, we are set free to pursue our own particular path of wisdom. This frees us from worry, leaving our minds clear. The clear mind then becomes an open channel[27] for greater understanding. The only thing that can hinder this flow of wisdom is emotional disturbance.

In past lives, the Jupiter retrograde individual seems to have understood these principles. She may not have practiced them fully or lived these beliefs. The house position of Lana's retrograde Jupiter shows that, for her, *living by faith* is a spiritual matter.

When Mercury is retrograde the general consciousness definition of a good mind does not fit the individual. Mercury is a perceptive tool and its vehicles are the senses. Retrograde Mercury has one or more expanded senses and thus is able to see, hear, or sense a great deal that the general population does not, and for which it has no words. Because the language of the early environment is not adequate to express what retrograde Mercury perceives, communication may be difficult and many choose between listening to the inner voice of their thoughts or the voices of those around them, simply because they cannot mesh the two. An observable effect is the individual who visibly seems to be searching for words when asked a question. This is similar to one who thinks in a language different from the one being spoken. In a sense that is precisely what individuals have to do when natal Mercury is retrograde. To them, all words have a broader meaning than the generally accepted one, and if they are to communicate effectively they will have to become aware that they speak from a different level of mind than many of the people around them.

Retrograde Mercury can lead to a great deal of loneliness and a feeling of alienation. Without communication, relationships are difficult to maintain and give little satisfaction.

For Lana this is compounded by the placement of her Mercury in Sagittarius, which means that she thinks in concepts and principles, and their applications. Even when direct, Sagittarius Mercury sometimes speaks over the heads of listeners.

Dynamics of Lana's Yod

The initial problem with Lana's Yod is one of communication and language. Notice that her third house of communication is Scorpio, suggesting the power of the word, which is the basic principle of creative consciousness.

Early in life she may be afraid to speak her word because of the changes she knows are needed. She may hold some subconscious fears of instituting change, left over from a previous incarnation. Given the quincunx to Mercury, the fear may be around words used or omitted.

Jupiter initially has difficulty around the issue of self-worth: "Does she feel worthy to speak the words?" She may also be short on money because of the self-worth issue.

---

[27]The author spontaneously began to channel information when Jupiter went retrograde by progression in her natal chart.

The Mercury foundation of this chart shows a questing mind—one that finds learning nearly as necessary as breathing. This will keep Lana on an eternal quest to resolve the early difficulties of the Yod, and the means of fulfilling its promise.

In mundane terms, the Uranus-Jupiter sextile may refer to a change for the better and, specifically, a financial improvement. This could allow her the freedom to express her gift for inspiring others through language—spoken, written, or broadcast. The whole process may well begin with learning a new language—not a traditional spoken and written language but the language of astrology,[28] computers, music, or metaphysics.

Above all else, Lana's major problem is that initially she has no language to adequately express what she knows intellectually and/or as channeled from higher mind. I think she will succeed because her Midheaven is in Gemini, the sign ruled by that very special Mercury. She has a message for the world, and I believe she will get the word out.

---

[28]These three planets are particularly apt for astrology. Metaphysics is likely to be more a matter of remembering than of learning.

Slingshot or Boomerang Yod
Quincunx, Sextile, Opposition

The slingshot or boomerang is a variation of the standard Yod, sometimes called a focused or motivated Yod. It differs from the standard in that it has a fourth planet that is 180 degrees from the Yod point on the midpoint of the sextile—splitting it into two semi-sextiles.

This Yod is a more complex version of the standard Yod. The reaction point is like a pressure valve and in some ways it makes it easier to release the pressure buildup found in a standard Yod. However, in some ways it is worse when the unevolved Yod lets off the energy in an uncontrolled or harmful fashion.

We may never feel in total control of our lives when we have a Yod in our charts. Life seems fated. We have to surrender to a higher power and sacrifice some personal desires and needs. Along the way we can at least move from the back seat up to the front passenger seat and start enjoying the ride.

John

John's Yod is comprised of Saturn in Capricorn quincunx retrograde Uranus in Leo quincunx the Sun in Pisces. Venus in Aquarius is opposition retrograde Uranus in Leo, semi-sextile Saturn and the Sun

Capricorn represents the outer limits of the current definition of the word "human." These general limits are the only limits that John has. Uranus in Leo may want to change or seem to change, but because it is retrograde, change is slow and difficult to do for many years. Saturn in the third house can be depressive, and its quincunx to retrograde Uranus adds a kind of hopelessness.

The Pisces Sun is at the (evolutionary) level of mastery. Although technically in the fourth house, it is so close to the next cusp as to be treated like it is in the fifth house; or we might read it as somewhat unconscious early in life but actively reaching for (verbal-Mercury) creativity later on. Again, the timing can be considered as delayed by the sluggish retrograde Uranus.

There is another factor: Venus in Aquarius, as the foundation planet and reason for incarnation. John's spiritual motivation is impersonal and unconditional love.

For John, this incarnation is clearly a volunteer one. He comes to Earth out of his great love for the planet and/or its inhabitants. However, entering at this particular time-space location, he is dropped into a much lower (vibration) consciousness-level than his own. The simple way to understand the difference is to say that at that level Aquarius is still ruled by Saturn, which keeps it at the limits of possibility. Still, with Sun (and Mercury) in Pisces, on some level John knows better. Its ruler is Neptune in Scorpio and powerful, with a retrograde rating to add the term Seeker to John's self-image/Ascendant.

More than that, John's unconditional love is a powerful motivator. In time, even though it takes time, Uranus will perform its ultimate job of breaking any too-strong Saturn limits. At that point, John will remember a better definition of Aquarius, under the new rulership of Uranus, as unlimited possibilities.

John's legacy to Earth is a demonstration of how truly impersonal love can change the world. The song below may well become the theme song of John's life!

If coal can turn to diamonds

And Sand can turn to pearls

If a worm can turn into a butterfly

Then love can change the world.

Three Interlocking Standard Yods
Sextile, Quincunx

When interpreting Ginnie's chart, which illustrates this Yod, we begin with the interception of Cancer-Capricorn, which means no-parenting.[29] The Sun is in Cancer and intercepted, and because it is ruled by the Moon, it behaves more like Pisces than Cancer. There was really only one parental figure, who was nominally both mother and father. That parent was too busy to parent Ginnie because she was more dedicated to the God/dess she served than to her mate and family. Some would say she was, "so Heaven bound as to be no Earthly good!"

The key quincunx is the forgotten twelfth house Pluto in aspect to the not-good or not-mine eighth house Moon. The Pisces Moon describes Ginnie's mother. Although too busy doing good works to notice the needs of her children and family, to outsiders she may have been a saint. The problem with that is that saints, being essentially impersonal, do not make good mothers.

Pluto in Leo may be pretend-power, or it may refer to the Father's power. What Ginnie may have thought and believed was that it was the power of God that took her mother's attention away from her child. She wanted no part of a power that took control of lives in that way; hence, her intent to forget (twelfth house) Pluto-power.

First Yod: Pluto, Midheaven, Moon

The twelfth house Pluto in Leo is quincunx the Taurus Midheaven and sextile the eighth house Moon in Pisces, which is quincunx Pluto. Ginnie's life-goal is represented by her Taurus Midheav-

---

[29]In most cases, *no parenting* actually refers to a single parent who must also be the financial support of the family. She (usually the mom) is much to busy to adequately nurture her child, who is left to grow up on her own. This is only as traumatic as the native believes it to be, since the Cancer-Capricorn interception is also *the mark of the Old Soul* and well able to rear herself.

Designs for a New Age

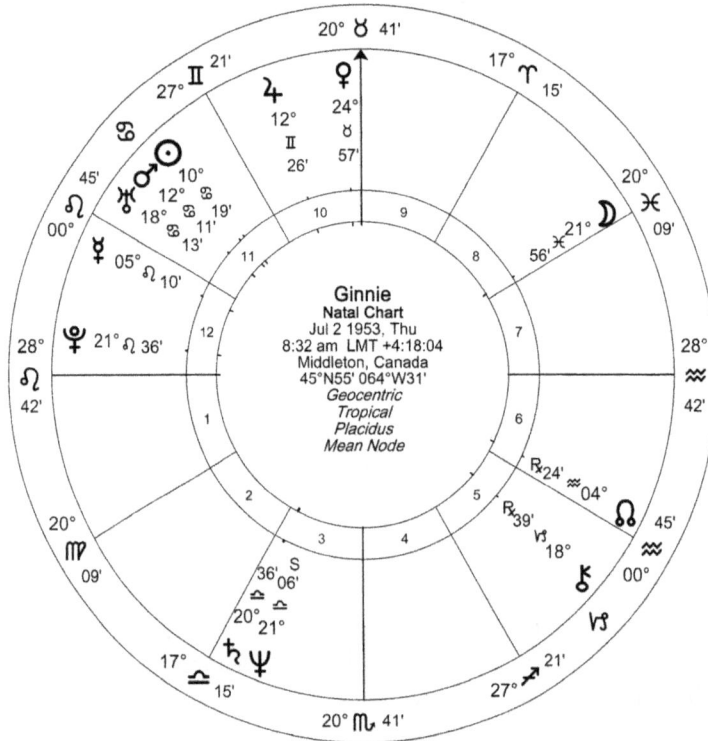

Ginnie
Natal Chart
Jul 2 1953, Thu
8:32 am LMT +4:18:04
Middleton, Canada
45°N55' 064°W31'
Geocentric
Tropical
Placidus
Mean Node

en conjunct Venus. She may want to be good and to have integrity, but she also wants money/affluence. Like her mother, she cares about people, but she knows the real meaning of the command to "love thy neighbor, as thyself," not more than myself, but in the same way as I love myself. The initial problem with this is that in forgetting her power she also forgets how to create an affluent life

Second Yod: Moon, Pluto, Chiron

The eighth house Pisces Moon is quincunx Pluto and retrograde Chiron in Capricorn, which is sextile the Moon.

The key to resolution for this chart is the retrograde Chiron intercepted in the fifth house of creativity. Some part of Chiron's task is always to upgrade the entire chart, expanding consciousness.

Another aspect of Chiron is choice. The interception of Chiron makes that choice seem unavailable until Ginnie is in her twenties, and most likely until her first Saturn return. Then, with choice available, the retrograde factor emerges as an absolute necessity to make a choice about Pluto power. No longer can it be forgotten. Ginnie must retrieve it and make it her own, for better or worse. This brings up the dilemma of the third Yod.

Third Yod: Moon, Pluto, Neptune

The eighth house Pisces Moon is quincunx Pluto in Leo and the Saturn-retrograde Neptune conjunction in Libra, which is sextile Pluto.

Saturn in Libra refers to shared boundaries, and points to a lack of separation from Ginnie's mother. Seemingly, it has always been *just the two of us, me and you.* Adding Neptune blurs this even further because the mother seemed to have no real boundaries either (Pisces doesn't).

This left Ginnie pulled in two directions emotionally, from the absorption of her need to sacrifice her life for the faith and her anger at her mother for sacrificing her childhood/infancy to the faith.

However, the saving grace of this is that Neptune is retrograde, which makes Ginnie a Seeker. She will ever seek truth; note Gemini/questioning with Jupiter *in the tenth house as a part of her life-goal.* In time she will realize that she and her mother are *equals* and *spiritual partners,* rather like twins separated by a generation.

Yod Configurations

The Golden or Magical Yod
Quintiles and Bi-quintiles

Quintiles are fifth harmonic aspects; the two-fifths aspects are bi-quintiles. The quintile (seventy-two degrees) is often shown on computer-generated horoscopes, but the companion bi-quintile (144 degrees) might not be. To be valid these aspects should contain no more than two to two and a half degrees of orb, or a total of five degrees in the Yod.

The number five has traditionally been linked to creativity and self-expression, and quintiles can be said to play a part in the grand design for life. At one level they permit expression of inherited creative talents. At a higher level they refer to our spiritual heritage, creative consciousness. Perhaps they represent the place where physical and spiritual genetics meet as self-expression. Five is also linked to play and the roles that we play in the great drama called life. They remind us that the role we play can, must, and will change as we mature.

The qualities of planets linked by quintile create most easily when we pretend that they have already done so. A deliberate use of acting talent for mental/magical creation can be highly successful for natives.

As a general practice it is recommended that all quintiles be regarded as positive aspects because they represent abilities or talents inherited from our own past lives. These can seem to be inherited from older family members, but that is probably as much a matter of soul affinity as genetics. At worst, quintiles offer us the opportunity to turn lemons into lemonade. They represent linked areas of life where our spirit will coax or drive us toward some creative activity or function.

Quintiles and bi-quintiles can teach us how to play our way through life, how to live effortlessly, how to let our light shine, and be true to our spiritual heritage. They allow us to rule our own life and to command what we want and need. In this place, if in no other area of the chart, we are hereditary rulers of life and heirs to the kingdom. We need to command, not plead. Our prayers should have the nature of requisitions from supplies that are already ours to claim.

A triangular pattern comprised of one quintile and two bi-quintiles forms a golden or magical Yod. It functions similarly to a standard Yod. As the inconjunct Yod deals in intellectual consciousness, so the quintile Yod is about creative consciousness. It might be treated as an implied pentagram in the sense that it becomes a place in which creativity flourishes and magic happens.

It represents three creative elements that offer mutual support to each other. They might be three facets or elements of the same creative flow.

At first some natives might attempt to choose between these talents, possibly trying each in turn without the expected amount of success. Only when synthesized would they would produce well and then usually quite magnificently.

Like the twelfth-harmonic Yod, this shows a (sometimes unconscious) single-minded purpose around which the remainder of the life moves. Since the task is often one which the ordinary person would not think of, the native can be confused or dismayed at the appearance of a compulsion that drives his or her life toward a specific application of these talents. It sometimes seems to have little regard for how the native (thinks that) she or he feels about it.

Like all Yods, this configuration contains the seeds of greatness because it is empowered by the very Hand of God. This writer does not consider these patterns to be destiny so much as a commitment made before entering incarnation. These are volunteers in the metaphysical army.

Lisa

Lisa's Scorpio Ascendant is quintile the Jupiter-IC conjunction in Capricorn, and both are bi-quintile the Gemini Chiron-South Node conjunction.

Astrologer is part of Lisa's[30] self image/Ascendant. A modern Mage (as in magi), Scorpio is also a natural psychologist. This is nicely supported by her Jupiter-IC conjunction in Capricorn, which is the foundation of her chart. From the third house side it suggests something learned—or relearned.

Jupiter also provides teaching skills as an inherent talent. Full manifestation, however, required Chiron, discovered in the sky during her fortieth year. During that same year she began to study astrology and that study provided the language/Gemini with which to express/fifth harmonic that which was inherently known.

Chiron comes from the eighth; although it was devalued in the world of her childhood, it was transformed as a major adult value. Only then did she notice a highly evolved linkage between right and left brain. At the keyboard she becomes a conscious channel—using the logical mind to tune in files of otherwise unconscious material through the intuitive function. Out of this comes the Gemini/books for Jupiter publication. Gradually her tenth house Pluto will become fully vested

---

[30]Lisa is actually Alice Miller, the author of this book.

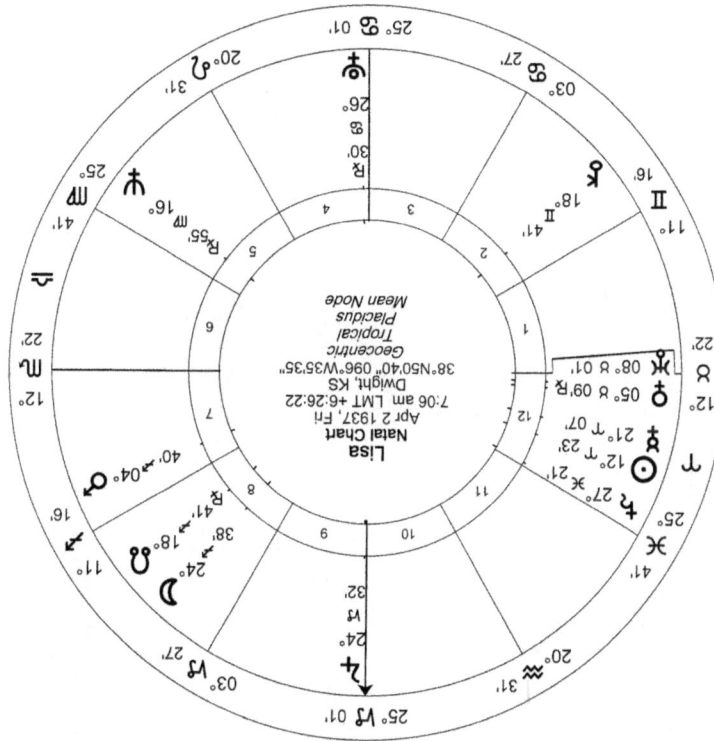

through the Scorpio Ascendant. The Yod represents the astrologer as consultant, teacher, and writer with output at the South Node of focused intention.[31]

---

[31]See *From the Nodes to Fortuna: Journey and Goal* by Rev. Alice Miller.

Yod Configurations

Attunement or Harmony Yod
Bi-septile and Tri-septile

Dividing a 360 degree circle by seven produces the septile group. The bi-septile is 102 degrees, and the tri-septile is 156 degrees.[32] These aspects always result in fractions of degrees, so they are hard to see. The approximate arcs are septile, 51° 26"; bi-septile, 102° 51"; and the tri-septile, 154° 17".

Seventh harmonic aspects have been largely ignored. They belong to a higher level of consciousness and being that is just beginning to become apparent on Earth. They are aspects of internal union and impersonal commitment, intended to leave a mark on the world.

Seven has several meanings. It is the sum of four/earth and three/spirit, or grounded spirituality. In life, the seventh harmonic is related to the capacity to live in the world but not of the world. At its most potent it refers to the inner marriage, the union of spirit and form that dissolves union into unity.

Seventh harmonic aspects are indications of the ability to use the planets or points linked by them in impersonal ways designed to affect reality. Energetically, they seem to work in series[33], beginning with the planet that is first after the Ascendant. Signs involved may show types of action, and the planets would show what parts of being would best cooperate in the process. The aspect would point to whether the need was for layering energy/septile, removing attention/bi-septile, or using word power/tri-septile to move energy from one place to another, through the combined use of affirmation and denial.

---

[32]These are approximate.

[33]Third and sixth harmonics work simultaneously, as a unity or a parallel circuit. They have no prerequisites, as seventh harmonics do.

Seventh harmonic linkages exist within us like musical chords waiting to be sounded. When the outer planets make transiting aspects to them, they reverberate, sometimes chaotically, leading to creative change in our lives. Uranian grace may step in, Neptunian disintegration may occur, or we may consciously invoke these processes through Plutonian (mental or physical) rituals. In these areas the self-realized individual may invoke the invisible power of life to lessen the chaos or the trauma of it. In such places we are compelled/Pluto to trust/Neptune in the graciousness/Uranus of life. Here we are linked to the invisible realm and must trust in the guidance and assistance that come from there. The Libra influence on septiles is transformed to that of the inner partner who shares our joys and sorrows and never abandons us—even when we forget or deny its existence.

Tommy

Tommy has Gemini-Sagittarius intercepted in the twelfth-first houses, so we know that he is in some way a messenger. This is further emphasized by the interception of Mercury.

Saturn intercepted in Sagittarius pictures ever-expanding boundaries or limits. With this intercepted/unconscious, Tommy takes it for granted as normal. As a consequence, it has taken time for him to realize that everybody cannot do the things that he can do.

The attunement Yod shows a smooth but somewhat unusual linkage between Mars, Moon, and Pluto.

Retrograde Mars provides the opportunity to see through human desire to the divine plan. It allows us to see life as pure energy in/as temporary form. Various techniques can be designed for stabilizing physical energy and for creating desirable, supportive physical objects and opportunities. To a large degree, this will be Pluto's task.

Mars is the spiritual form that needs of the Spirit take. Our desires are what our Deity wants us to have. When retrograde, Mars in Taurus refers to divine supply brought over from previous incarnations. It may well be regarded as treasures laid up in heaven, banked assets available for use during the current lifetime.

Moon in Aquarius converts the Solar Purpose from a personal to an impersonal one. Having graduated from the karmic wheel, natives are on a mission to Earth. Their energy channel has evolved to galactic dimensions. Where earlier Moons converted solar energy for personal use, this one channels divine energy[34] to Earth. Galactic ambassadors, their lives are invested in meeting the needs of human survival and evolution. They channel inspiration and possibilities designed to change lives. They are not so much prophets, as prophecies.

Uranus-ruled Aquarian souls are meant to change the shape of reality. Whether aware of it or not, they work entirely in the realm of consciousness, from inspiration. Their solar energy is directed to the task of evolution and change. Some have no common sense. They do, however, have uncommon sense. Their lives are absolutely logical and rational but run on a different frequency,

---

[34]From the *Central Sun*, the center of the Universe, possibly by tapping the photon belt.

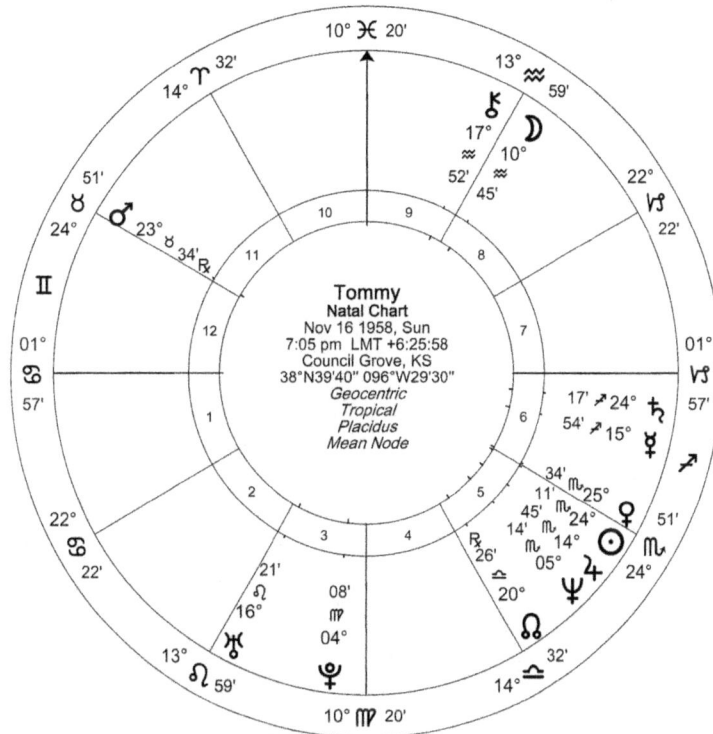

Tommy
Natal Chart
Nov 16 1958, Sun
7:05 pm LMT +6:25:58
Council Grove, KS
38°N39'40" 096°W29'30"
Geocentric
Tropical
Placidus
Mean Node

guided by a different set of scientific laws.

The Aquarius Moon refers to a Soul that has outgrown the current definition of the word human. Aquarius is more than (merely) man. He stands between Earth and Heaven, linking the two as a priest. In this Yod, the priest is also an alchemist.

Virgo refers to one perfect, whole, and complete, neither damaged nor ill. It is the point where we take what we have learned and put it to use, choosing a work or service as our contribution to Life. Pluto in Virgo refers to newly perfected personal power. Tommy came to Earth with the assets of Mars and Moon fully developed, and able to support his life. This gives him the freedom to truly learn the use of personal power in daily life. He may be regarded as a newly-ordained priest and alchemist.

Tommy is a money-magician. He has been highly successful in the computer industry, almost from his teens. Chiron in his ninth house marks a decision to change his tenth house goals. About the time of his Chiron return, he got serious about a long-deferred avocation as a writer of futuristic fiction.

As he continues to write, we expect to see evidence of channeled material that is really prophecy. The intent hovers over the pages of his early books.

Designs for a New Age

Transformation Yod
Square, Sesquiquadrate

Eighth harmonic aspects are called quadrates. They are based on a division of the 360 degree circle into eighths. Six of them are included as squares and oppositions. The two remaining are the semi-square (forty-five degrees) and the sesquiquadrate (135 degrees).

As the inconjuncts relate to Mercury, so the quadrates relate to Venus, saying something like "I don't like you" or "You are not good enough." Sesquiquadrate planets/points hold negative judgments on each other. These judgments are usually inherited as subliminal attitudes absorbed very early in life and internalized as facts of life.

Quadrates have an appearance of "that's just the way it is," which is difficult to overcome. As consciousness rises in the general population, they become self-fulfilling prophecies. By our belief in the judgments, we create their proof. Until we resolve them, they cause difficulties in our social relationships (especially marital ones).

Quadrates are elements that "force" us to really look at how we compare to and/or differ from others. We may then claim the principles without claiming the ways in which another uses them, or without feeling that someone has stolen something from us or invaded our space or is copying our style.

The semi-square represents the "not-good" because the two ends will not integrate. They are disloyal and will not stick together, causing schisms in the family and in the internal structure. Some are sextile by sign which means that they can communicate, but the semi-square aspect derails the possibility due to a programed belief about the incompatibility of the two planetary principles.

Applied practically, this means that if you accept the good at one end of the semi-square, you will be denied the good in the other end. Some rather prevalent ideas in this area are those that suggest that to be truly spiritual, you must live celibate and/or in poverty. Another is the idea of the starving artist; this one requires choosing between developing talents and having financial security.

Jennie

Jennie's Sun stands alone, the only Gemini planet in her chart, and she has three planets and the South Node in Taurus. She has two jobs, working as a homemaker and in the home-building industry with her husband (Sun conjunct the Descendant, and the Pisces Moon in the fourth house).

Jennie's Yod is comprised of Saturn in Cancer square Chiron in Aries, with both sesquiquadrate retrograde Neptune in Sagittarius. The Gemini solar energy is channeled through her Pisces Moon, she has a Sagittarius Ascendant that is widely conjunct retrograde Neptune.

Jennie belongs to the earliest group of New Kids, born some eleven years before Chiron's discovery, and perhaps fifteen years before the first New Kids were recognized. Chiron seems to have remained invisible/unconscious in her life until at least her mid-teens, a kind of null point that could either help or hinder the other planets in the Yod or her fifth house.

Saturn in Cancer is in the eighth house (the child's not-mine house), suggesting a lack of protection and/or such fluctuating/fluid boundaries that she could never know the rules, much less obey

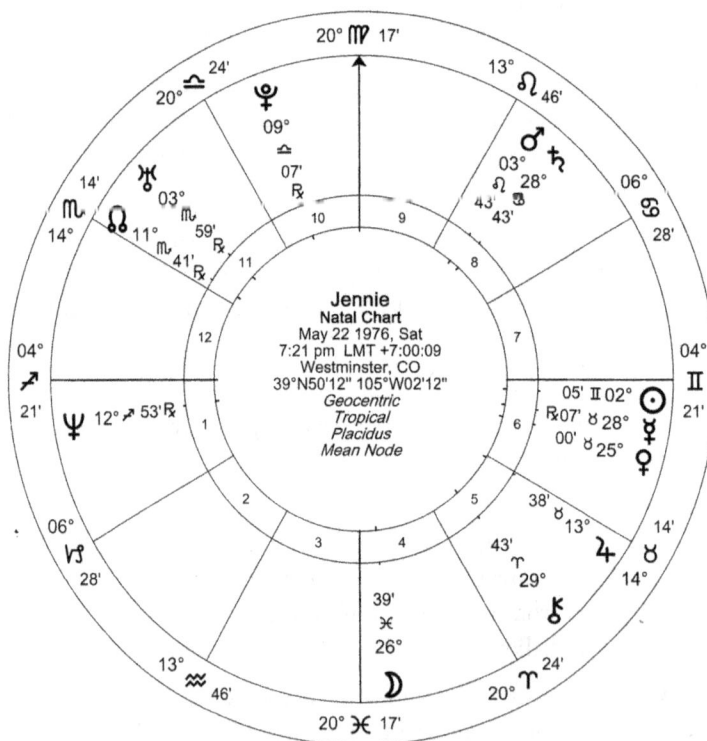

Jennie
Natal Chart
May 22 1976, Sat
7:21 pm LMT +7:00:09
Westminster, CO
39°N50'12" 105°W02'12"
Geocentric
Tropical
Placidus
Mean Node

them. This may have triggered Mars in Leo to produce some rather dramatic and justified anger, causing her to act out, possibly even to the point of rage. Anger/rage is incompatible with her Ascendant and Neptune; it steals energy from the rising conjunction.

Retrograde Neptune is a Seeker and quite compatible with the natural Sagittarian goal of expanding consciousness. However, for some years it may express as abandonment/Sagittarius and confusion/Neptune. But the secret of Neptune, the truth that Jennie searches for, is revealed by her foundation sign/Pisces and planet/Moon. Before all else, Jennie is a Master/Pisces Soul/Moon, and she chose this incarnation, knowing that she could trust her mastery to get her through whatever happened.

At some point Chiron would become conscious and her status as an upgraded human would be revealed. Around the same time, she would realize that the eighth house taboos are only forbidden or denied to children. Claiming her adulthood, she can claim the protection/Saturn of the outreaching/Mars role/Leo that she came to play on Earth. At that point Neptune s mastery will apply to the Sagittarius teacher/messenger. Ultimately she will serve/Virgo Midheaven others/Libra in powerful/Plutonian ways. The presence of Fortuna in the tenth will surely bring her great rewards, most likely after her Chiron return.

Another Transformation Yod

Occasionally we see a little Yod formation, or small T-square, comprised of two semi-squares and one square. Here the judgments held in the semi-squares are responsible for the disruptiveness of the square. Releasing the judgments will allow a synthesis of the two factors in square relationship. This releases power from the hindrance of the square, producing a high quality of creative potential at the point of the Yod.

Yod Configurations

Gestation Yod
Novile, Quarto-novile, Quarto-novile

Ninth harmonic aspects are called noviles, and sometimes nonagens, or noniles. In the series we find the novile at forty degrees, the bi-novile at eighty degrees, and the quarto-novile at 160 degrees. We also see semi-noviles (twenty degrees) and 140 degree combinations. These should be allowed no more than one to one and a half degrees orb.

These aspects have been interpreted in Hindu astrology as what life produces in the long run. Relating this to the Eastern belief in Nirvana—a point of nothingness, void, or absolute stillness—this aspect may refer to the ability or need to achieve that state relative to the planets or points involved in the aspect. In the West we may interpret this as an aspect of acceptance, even resignation.

Wholly impersonal, the aspect is truly active only in those committed to the good of the whole. Activity around it is out of our conscious control, mandated by the master plan to which we are committed and the resistance in the general consciousness which surrounds us.

Translation of the novile aspect involves numerology in horoscope interpretation. Forty is a number often used symbolically in Judeo-Christian scriptures. In each case, the period referred to equals a void time or a period of passage. We think specifically of the forty years spent in the wilderness between Egyptian slavery and the entrance into the Promised Land by the Children of Israel. This presents an image of the period of feeling lost that follows each time our consciousness shifts to the next level. Here we see the chosen people—those set apart for higher things—removed from the security of a parental monarchy in order to pioneer a new way of life. The metaphysical symbol is that of journeying to a new level of individuation—a metamorphosis in consciousness. The wilderness journey is gestation; the battle to claim the promised land is the labor period.

Another instance is that of Jesus spending forty days in the wilderness immediately after his baptism.[35] Before assuming his role as Messiah, he went through a dry spell, a period of silence, during which he accepted and made peace with his pre-incarnational commitment. He faced the temptation to use his power for world domination, choosing instead to teach others how to claim their own power.

The two events mentioned above might be viewed as gestation periods that preceded a rebirth of a nation in the first instance and of an individual in the second. More universally relevant is the forty-week-period of human gestation, which can be regarded as a principle of emergence. Whether a birth or a rebirth is experienced, gestation occurs silently, in the dark.

When it is a rebirth, in that darkness an old form seems to die as it is converted back to energy, then reformulated into a new, improved model. The novile calls attention to the cocoon stage of metamorphosis.

Of the nine actual planets, Pluto is the ninth, and in one aspect nine represents the ongoing cycles of life as preserved through metamorphosis. We are reminded that life is eternal and death is not an end. We shall be born again, like the butterfly who lives one life on the ground and a second in the sky within a single lifetime.

Ninth harmonic aspects point to destined transformations. They are destined because they come at specific points in our evolutionary journey. They are also choices and commitments because the journey to higher consciousness can only be the result of a spiritual contract. One can always see more from a higher elevation. Greater awareness *is* greater power. It is the apocalyptic revelation that is designed to transform our lives as dramatically as the transformation from a worm to a butterfly.

The Novile Yod

Ninth Harmonic, or novile Yods, are quite rare. They point to an incarnation committed to raising consciousness in Self and/or Others. That commitment forces ritualistic behavior designed to rewrite our early conditioning. This may then permit mysterious and/or magical revelations. New elements of power enter Earth, fostered by a type of procreative process at the nonphysical level.

However, in practice a novile Yod cannot be made to work in the environmental context. It demands a break with the past. Until that happens, natives struggle to move forward, while dragging the past behind them. Hauling it along drains energy and depletes and delays our creativity and/or spiritual commitment. Unlike other aspects, no compromise is possible with the novile. The only solution is to accept defeat and let go of our conditioning around them, irrevocably and permanently. There is something of the burnt offering about these Yods as we lay our frustration and defeat on a symbolic altar, allowing the fire to release energy from the old, to become potential substance of the new.

---

[35]Matt. 3:13 through 4:11.

These Yods suggest specific problems to be overcome. They warn of the resistance-factor in any creative, procreative, or generative union. Resistance between the factors in the aspect is intended to become a positive factor, driving the native to higher realizations. When that resistance is too strong, too sustained, the destined metamorphosis will never complete and the butterfly will die unborn.

When all goes well, the intensity of that resistance attracts attention to it, which generates questions. Those questions, in turn, attract answers. Those answers bring enlightenment, proving the existence of unseen elements in life.

At that point the measure of their dysfunction, relative to the houses, is the measure of their efficiency when released from the realm of conditioned response. When applied to our incarnational purpose, they become true power points, sometimes dancing for joy!

Morrie

Morrie was a man born too far ahead of his time. Life never gave him the space or support needed to fulfill his potential. The incredible resistance he met smothered the great potential of his Sagittarius New Moon, leaving it forgotten in his twelfth house. I met him at the time of his retirement. Perhaps one or both of us thought that I could help him resurrect his long-forgotten

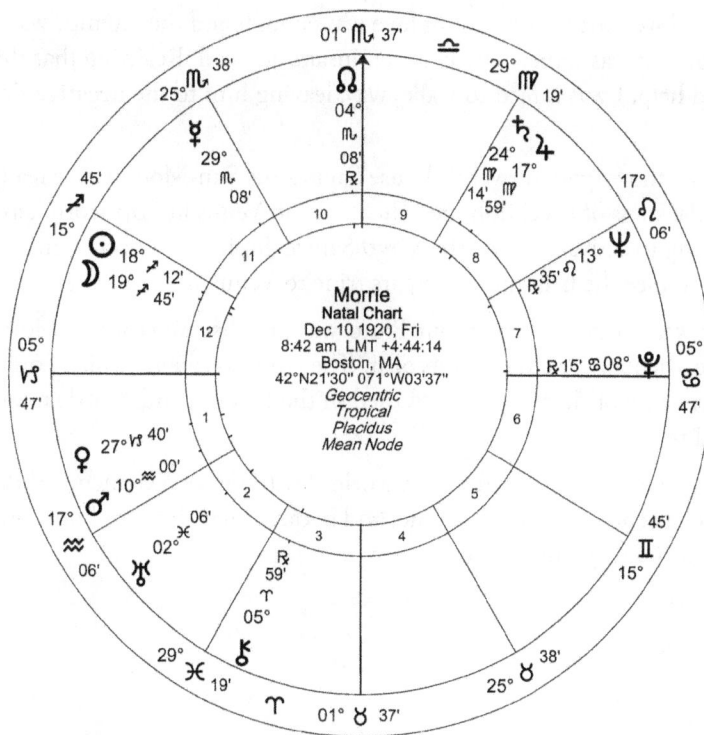

pre-incarnational commitment. If so, our reach exceeded our grasp.

Morrie's childhood was a horror story. Clearly his mother was less than sane, for she hated her boy. He told about trying to stay out of reach when he had to pass by her because any time he got close enough she hit him. The fact that he survived his childhood was in spite of her, not because of her. There were no stories about his biological father. While he was still quite small, a stepfather who was mob-connected entered the picture. Morrie seemed proud of that, perhaps pleased that this man was one person over which his mother had no power.

In the background, behind his gestation Yod, Morrie had an Aries-Libra interception—the only negative one that I have seen. Rather than a whole being, Morrie had nearly become a non-being. He seemed to have concluded that he was undesirable, unwanted, a necessary evil. Life had taught him that survival depended on his ability to steal energy. Having been widowed months earlier, when we met he was looking for another mate. Undoubtedly part of the attraction was my own positive Aries-Libra interception, which tends to generate, and often spill, high levels of energy.

By the time he reached adulthood, Morrie's mother had knocked all the spirit out of him. He had accepted a definition of himself as just another higher animal, a survivalist of the most danger-ous kind. His *need* was powerfully magnetic.

Morrie's idea of relationship was that of host-parasite. On some level I think I realized that my only protection was love. But no amount of love was enough and the attempt was simply enabling continued behavior that was somewhere between insane and evil. Realizing that this man was dan-gerous and beyond help, I was forced to walk away, leaving him to the negative side of Sagittarius: abandonment.

In Morrie's chart, the forgotten twelfth house Sagittarius Sun-Moon never really emerged from the psychological darkness of his childhood. The novile to Venus in Capricorn kept him struggling for forty years, trying to activate it, but the Virgo Saturn-Jupiter had been denied the child he was and it could not produce the help implied by its trine to Venus.

The Yod point was Pluto in Cancer, but Pluto was not discovered until Morrie was ten years old, so he never learned any real definition of it. The empowerment, which could have been his, had he been born twenty or thirty years later, died in the cocoon, and Morrie never grew beautiful wings, nor learned to fly.

And yet, perhaps he did leave a gift to the world, for there were elements of our time together that over the years have proved valuable to me, and because they did, this book, and several others, can be viewed as our joint gift to the world.

Thank-you Morrie.

www.ingramcontent.com/pod-product-compliance
Lightning Source LLC
Chambersburg PA
CBHW050013110426
42741CB00038B/3410